Their Fifteen Minutes

✦

Biographical Sketches of the Lindbergh Case

Mark W. Falzini

iUniverse, Inc.
New York   Bloomington

Their Fifteen Minutes
Biographical Sketches of the Lindbergh Case

iUniverse books may be ordered through booksellers or by contacting:

iUniverse
1663 Liberty Drive
Bloomington, IN 47403
www.iuniverse.com
1-800-Authors (1-800-288-4677)

ISBN: 978-0-595-52253-8 (pbk)
ISBN: 978-0-595-62309-9 (ebk)

Printed in the United States of America

For
Gregg Senko, Oliver Sissman, Siglinde Rach
& Dolores Raisch

To speak the name of the dead is to make them live again
--Ancient Egyptian Proverb

Contents

Illustrations

Preface

One day in late September 2007 I met with Harry Kazman, the author and producer of the annual Hauptmann Trial re-enactment in Flemington, New Jersey. We were discussing the book I had published a few years earlier, *Letters Home*, about the experiences of my mother's family while they were stationed in Occupied Germany after the Second World War. Harry then suggested a topic for a second book: "I think you should write a 'What ever happened to' style book about the Lindbergh Case." I looked at him like he was crazy but he persisted. He reminded me that we are both constantly asked, "what ever happened to so-and-so?" When I suggested that *he* should write the book, he laughed and said, "but *you* actually know the answers!" I told him I would think about it.

I pushed the idea to the back of my mind, but it was brought to the front again when I saw Harry the following month at the re-enactment. "I still say you ought to write that book." During my ride home from Flemington I thought about it some more and finally decided that I would give it a shot.

This is a unique book about the Lindbergh Kidnapping Case in that it does not put forth a theory and does not proclaim Hauptmann innocent or guilty. Rather it is a biographical reference book, hopefully filling in some blanks and providing what actors refer to as the "back story" to the characters that appear in all of the other books written about the case. I also see it as an opportunity to remind readers that the people connected to the case were just that – *people*.

The Lindbergh Case is a very complicated topic so that when authors write about it they must focus only on the aspects of peoples' lives that are directly connected to the case. Had they not been touched by history, many of the people in this book would have been unknown to most of us. Because they are connected to the Lindbergh Case, they live on. But they live on only partially because the rest of their life experiences are generally unknown to even the most avid researcher. As you will see in the pages that follow, there was more to their lives and careers than just the Lindbergh Case.

Many of the documents used in the research of this book, including many of the newspaper articles, can be found in the Lindbergh Kidnapping Archive of the New Jersey State Police Museum and Learning Center in West Trenton, New Jersey. The archive is the hub of Lindbergh Kidnapping Case research. Its collections of over 250,000 documents and countless photographs, not to mention videos, scrapbooks and the evidence from the Hauptmann Trial are all freely accessible to the public without charge. The reader is *strongly* urged to avail him or herself of these files.

Sadly, I was not able to include in this book everyone that I wanted to. Some of the people were so remote that, even with access to the vast archival collections at the State Police and elsewhere, it has not been possible for me to gather enough information about them. Often their obituaries dwelt extensively on their connection to the Lindbergh Case barely mentioning anything else about their lives.

On the other hand, I deliberately chose not to include Charles and Anne Lindbergh as well as Richard and Anna Hauptmann because their lives are already well known from existing Lindbergh Kidnapping literature and, in the case of the Lindberghs, from their own extensive biographies and autobiographies. I chose not to include Manfred Hauptmann, Anna and Richard's son. He has fought strenuously over the years to maintain his privacy and I wish to respect that.

I also reluctantly decided against including Hauptmann's attorney, Edward J. Reilly and New York Police Detective James J. Finn mainly because there are already two excellent biographies recently published about them. Therefore, to learn more about Edward J. Reilly, I would highly recommend the St. John's University School of Law Journal article, *Owls Shouldn't Claw at Eagles: Big Ed Reilly and the Lindbergh Kidnapping Case* by William H. Manz. His article provides a very detailed account of Reilly's career, involvement in the Lindbergh Case and, most interestingly, Reilly's bout with syphilis, his committal to a mental hospital and his divorce just months before he died. (New York State Bar Association, June 2005. Volume 77, No 5).

For the biography of James J. Finn, I would direct the reader to the June 2005 issue of "American History" for Barry Levy's biography of Finn entitled, *Cracking the Lindbergh Case.* (American History Magazine, Volume 40 No. 2. June 2005).

Both of these biographies are on file at the State Police Museum in West Trenton, New Jersey.

Their Fifteen Minutes: Biographical Sketches of the Lindbergh Case is a collection of essays, each one standing independent of the others. It is a reference book that does not need to be read cover to cover. It should be noted that the subjects covered in each essay or chapter are not presented in any particular order; in this book no one person has importance over any other. All of the stories end pretty much the same way: "And then they died." Death is, after all, the great equalizer.

I wrote this book so that the lives of the people contained herein would not be forgotten. And maybe, once you have read about them, you will come to have a better appreciation about who they really were and how the Lindbergh Kidnapping Case not only affected their lives but how their lives may have impacted the Case. As you will see, there was much more to them than just their fifteen minutes of fame.

Mark W. Falzini
West Trenton, NJ
Spring 2008

Acknowledgements

I am indebted to a great number of people who have both directly and indirectly contributed to the publication of this book. First and foremost, I owe a great deal of thanks to the late Thomas Faughnan of the Trenton State College History Department. He was my mentor while I was a history major there and I was fortunate to have taken a class with him during every semester but one.

If not for Harry Kazman, I never would have had the idea of writing a book of mini-biographies of people involved with the Lindbergh Case. I thank him for planting the seed that has grown into this book.

In short, I owe everything to Dolores Raisch. If not for Dolores, this book would not have been possible and most definitely I would not be where I am today in my career. Dolores took me under her wing when, in 1992, as a young man fresh out of college, I first started working at the New Jersey State Police Museum.   She taught me not only about the Lindbergh Case but more importantly how to actually find things the voluminous files. If not for her, when it came time to "sink or swim" I would definitely have sank to the bottom.

Siglinde Rach is another without whom I would have great difficulty in doing my job. She is a font of information and is by far the best researcher – of any topic – that I have ever known. She is a dear friend on whom I can always call for help. She is also a great proofreader and fact checker! If there are any mistakes in this book, it's because I didn't listen to her.

I want to thank my cousin, Christiane Hawkshaw, for introducing me to Ian Waller of Link Line Ancestral Research in Luton, England. He did a wonderful job tracking down Violet Sharp's family information for me. Suzanne Nurnberg is another great genealogist who specializes in New

Jersey records. She has been a great help in both my own personal genealogy as well as tracking down information about some of the people mentioned in this book.

I am grateful to Major Hugo Stockburger for his friendship and trusting me to ensure that his legacy is protected, for the interviews and for his willingness to entrust the history of the State Police with me.

Steve Lehmann has been a good friend over the years and I am grateful to him for providing his research on Betty Gow to me and to the State Police Museum archive. Pat Hartman of Our Saviour Lutheran Church in Mobile, Alabama was very kind in providing me information about Hans and Maria Müller. Jeannette Cafaro and Eileen Morales of the Princeton Historical Society helped with information on the Matthews Construction Company and Michael Melsky provided me copies of numerous obituaries from the *New York Times*. All of this material is on file at the State Police Museum.

I am deeply indebted to my very good friend Petter Myhr Næss of Oslo, Norway who tracked down Red Johnson's daughter for me and arranged for me to not only meet her but to visit all of the locations in Norway associated with Red and his family. In that regard I am also very grateful to Elsie Marie Johnsen for agreeing to meet me and to share her father's life story. Thor Vigne of Norway was also helpful in tracking down locations related to Johnson, including where he is buried.

The children of William Allen (William Jr., Gerald, Elinor and Elizabeth) have been incredibly kind to me ever since we first met in 2006 and as I researched their father's life and they were very eager to share any information they had with me. They have accepted me as one of their family and for that I am grateful.

My friend, the late Thelma Miller, donated her entire scrapbook collection to the State Police Museum and it was in her 17 volumes that I was able to find many newspaper articles that helped me in the researching of this book. Her collection is an incredible resource of the "cultural history" of the Lindbergh Case that I highly recommend to future researchers.

I owe special thanks to my friend Wayne McDaniel who spent several days helping me trying to come up with a title for this book.

I would also like to thank Curtis Leeds of the Hunterdon County Democrat, Richard Sloan, Lloyd Gardner, Bill Mooney, Kurt Tolksdorf, Kevin Klein, Ian Tregillis, Oliver Sissman, Gregg Senko, Joe Wurtz, Tom Cavallo, Linda Kale and especially my mother Barbara Falzini for their encouragement and strong support as I worked on this book.

Lastly, I must mention my aunt, Judith Engster Kale, because she told me that she has always wanted her name in a book. Here it is!

Introduction[1]

In 1927, the American people were in desperate need of a hero. Our nation was suffering through the moral and political corruption brought about by prohibition and the exploits of organized crime. There was a sense of hopelessness in an age where virtues such as honesty, courage, and pride in achievements seemed impossible to recognize. Charles A. Lindbergh never planned to be a hero when he decided to accept the challenge of a French businessman named Raymond Orteig.

Lindbergh was a young airmail pilot who, at the age of 25, decided to compete for the first non-stop flight between New York and Paris. Others had tried before him, meeting failure and even death. On May 20, 1927, fighting heavy odds and bad weather, Lindbergh took off from Roosevelt Field in New York in his monoplane named "The Spirit of St. Louis. " He flew alone, non-stop, across the Atlantic Ocean for 33-1/2 hours before landing at Le Bourget Field in Paris, France on May 21, 1927. His daring accomplishment won him not only the $25,000 prize, but also worldwide recognition and fame. It cost him, however, a loss of privacy that would last a lifetime.

Following his famous flight, Lindbergh made many "good-will" flights to set new records and advance the cause of aviation. While in Mexico on one such tour, he met Anne Morrow, daughter of the United States Ambassador to Mexico, Dwight Morrow. Charles and Anne were married in a private ceremony at her parents' home in Englewood, New Jersey, on May 27, 1929. Their first child, a son, was born on Anne's 24th birthday, June 22, 1930. They named him Charles A. Lindbergh, Jr.

In the winter of 1932, the young family had not quite settled in their newly built home near Hopewell, New Jersey when their lives would change forever. On the evening of March 1, 1932, Charles A. Lindbergh, Jr. was kidnapped as he slept in his nursery crib. Several clues were left behind including a ransom note and a homemade three-section ladder and a chisel. That night the New Jersey State Police began their investigation into the crime that shocked and outraged America and the world.

An intermediary named John F. Condon, entered the case after offering his assistance through a newspaper ad and met with the kidnapper on two occasions. In all, 15 ransom notes were received during the course of the negotiations. Lindbergh insisted on paying the $50,000 ransom demanded in the original ransom note, believing this was the only way to get his son back. Following the instructions of the kidnapper, the ransom was handed over by Condon on April 2, 1932, in a Bronx cemetery. The serial numbers of these bills, some of which were gold certificates, were carefully listed, although this fact was not made public. The baby's body, however, was discovered on May 12, 1932 several miles from his Hopewell home.

Investigators from the New Jersey State Police, United States Department of Justice (presently, the Federal Bureau of Investigation) and the United States Treasury Department were busy pursuing every possible lead. In addition, analysis of the wood used in the construction of the kidnap ladder would offer valuable clues once a suspect was apprehended. Handwriting experts carefully examined the 15 ransom notes and this, too, would prove informative and revealing.

In September 1934, at a New York service station, a man paid for his gasoline with a $10.00 gold certificate. The United States had officially gone off the gold standard in May 1933, and the station attendant did not want to risk the bank refusing the gold certificate. For this reason, he wrote the purchaser's license number on the $10. 00 bill. This lead broke the case when an alert bank teller notified the authorities of the gold certificate. The serial number matched with one that appeared on the list of Lindbergh ransom money serial numbers. The license number was traced to Bruno Richard Hauptmann who lived in the Bronx section of New York. Hauptmann was arrested on September 19, 1934 at which time another ransom bill was found in his wallet. The following day $13,760 of the ransom money was found in Hauptmann's garage. A floorboard in Hauptmann's attic was found to match the wood used for one of the rails in the kidnap ladder. Handwriting samples were taken from Hauptmann and found by experts to match the writing of the ransom notes. He was extradited from New York to New Jersey to be tried in the state and county in which the crime occurred.

Hauptmann's trial began January 2, 1935 in Flemington, New Jersey. Physical evidence, as well as expert and eyewitness testimony directly connected him to the ladder, the handwriting in the ransom notes, and possession of the ransom money. The evidence and testimony presented at the six-week trial led to Hauptmann's conviction of murder during the commission of a felony. The sentence was death by electrocution. Following unsuccessful appeals and controversial intervention by the Governor, Bruno Richard Hauptmann was executed in Trenton, New Jersey on April 3, 1936. Just prior to his execution, Hauptmann declared that "They think when I die, the case will die. They think it will be like a book I close. But the book, it will never close."

1. Red Johnson[2]

The morning after the infamous Crime of the Century occurred, Henry "Red" Johnson set out on a road trip from Englewood, New Jersey to his brother's home in Connecticut. The next day, March 3rd, he was arrested in Hartford becoming the first "prime suspect" in the case. Johnson was the boyfriend of the child's nanny, Betty Gow. He was also an illegal immigrant from Norway.

After a thorough investigation, the police eventually exonerated Red Johnson from any involvement in the kidnapping and he was sent back to Norway. He disappeared from public view and was not heard from again.

Born on November 28, 1905 in *Reier, Jeløya*, Moss, Norway, Finn Henrik (Henry) Johansen was 5 feet 7 ¾ inches tall, of medium build with blue eyes. Because of his chestnut-red hair, he was known as *Rødejohnson* – Red Johnson. He did not mind the nickname that he carried all his life: "He didn't care because [in] the town of Moss everybody had [nicknames]. The rest of his family were called 'the carpenters' or 'the tailors' because many of my grandfather's brothers were tailors…and my father was 'Red Johnson the Carpenter.' Almost everybody had nicknames."

Moss is a medium-size town located 50 minutes southeast of Oslo in *Østfeld* County. The town, known for having more hours of daylight than any other part of Norway, traces its history back to the Stone and Bronze Ages.

Moss takes its name from the Mors River, on which it was founded in the 14th Century. By the mid 1500s, the town had become a busy coastal town with sawmills and shipyards. Farming was another main activity and "as early as in the 1600s, Moss had a number of large farming estates." *Reier*, where Red Johnson was born, is one such estate located on the *Jeløya* peninsula. Known as the "Gem of the *Oslofjord*…the western part of *Jeløya*

1

has exceptionally beautiful scenery…Today large parts of *Jeløya* are protected areas and…consist of protected beech forests with a network of beautiful walking paths."

Red's father, Henrik Johansen, moved from *Rygge* to Moss and in October 1899 he married Bertha Josephine Olsen. From 1899 until circa 1904 they lived with Henrik's parents – Johan and Andrea Andersen – at *Bråtengate* 20. Two of Red's siblings – Claudia and Erling Fredrik – were born here. The family then moved to the nearby *Reier* estate and it was here that Red was born in November 1905.

Red's mother, Bertha Josephine, was born in 1874 in Moss, the daughter of Frederik and Anette Marie Olsen. "She was a very nice person and was deeply religious. But she also had made up her own mind [about things]… I could go to her and my father could go to her and we could talk about anything and she was always open to [our] thoughts."

Red's father was also a very religious man. He belonged to a cult known as "*Guds Forsamlilng*" or "*Guds Menisghed*" – God's Congregation – an offshoot of the Methodist church in Norway. A fisherman by trade, he had money and owned fishing boats that he kept in a boatyard on *Sjøgata* – a street parallel to *Bråtengate*. The family was, however, a poor family because he turned over all of his income at this time to his religious community.

> My grandmother got so little money from him: they had not much food and she was tending ten children alone because he was away all week. And she sat up nights and sewed clothes for all these children and for other people to earn some money. And he had money that he gave away to that [religious] society.

Henrik Johansen was a very strict father – a hard man who was away all week on his fishing boat. He would return to his family only on the weekends and when he did, his children had to line up in order of age and he would proceed to beat each one of them. "They all got a beating because either they had done something wrong during the week or they would come to do it the next week when he was away."

By the early 1920s, two of his sons – Erling Fredrik (Fred) and Arne Johan (John) – had had enough of the weekly beatings and left Norway for America. "Before they went to America they took their father up to the attic and they beat him up and then left the house, came to America and never came back to Norway again."

When Henrik Johansen died sometime prior to 1935, the family was relieved. "Nobody talked about him. He was called Henrik and if they said something it was always 'Ptui! Henrik' and nothing more."

While Red was growing up, he was very clever in school. He received the highest grades and he wanted to continue his studies. His grades were so good that in the early 1920s the community offered him a scholarship for university. "But his father wouldn't have that. He was not allowed to go and study. And he got angry and went to America…"

Prior to immigrating to America, Red Johnson took a position as a seaman on the *S/S Topdalsfjord*. Canadian Vickers LTD in Montreal built this 4,271-ton ship in 1921.

Red first visited the United States on September 9, 1923. In March 1927, the ship returned to the United States, docking in Brooklyn, New York. It was here that he "jumped ship" and remained illegally in the country.

He lived temporarily with his brother Fred in Brooklyn while working in the shipyard of Jacobsen Peterson. On May 20, 1927 – the day Charles Lindbergh took off on his famous transatlantic flight – Red began working on the yacht of Alfred P. Sloan, Jr.

This job lasted until October, when he began a three-month vacation in Marlboro, Maine, at the home of his aunt and uncle, Mr. and Mrs. Arthur Johnson. He then visited his brother, John, in West Hartford, Connecticut.

In January 1928, Red began working on the Inter-Borough Subway while living with the Carpenter family on Simpson Street in the Bronx. He held this job until May when he was hired to work on Arthur Levine's small yacht. He switched to the yacht of Leroy Frost of Nyack, New York, in August of that year and worked for him until he was laid off in October.

Red now lived temporarily at the Thompson residence on 8th Avenue in Brooklyn until he began work on the yacht *Ibis*, owned by the Christie family of Hastings-on-the-Hudson. He quit this job on Christmas Eve, 1928. Returning by train to New York City, he once again took up residence with the Thompson family of Brooklyn remaining there until the following May.

In January or February 1929, Red filed an application with the U. S. Consul in Oslo, Norway, for proper entrance into the United States. "In April 1931 I received another letter from the United States Consul at Oslo informing me to come to the American Consulate at Oslo on April 7, 1931, but I did not receive the letter in time to permit me to arrive there on that date…Meanwhile, my mother in Moss, Norway, arranged to have my application deferred."

February 15, 1929 was Red's first day of employment on McKnight Mitchell's yacht, *The Flying Myst*. In May of that year, they sailed on Long

Island Sound. Red held this job until he quit on November 15. Remaining in Brooklyn for the winter, he lived on 83rd street, holding various "odd jobs."

From April until October 1930, Red worked on Thomas W. Lamont's yacht, *Reynard*. Thomas Lamont was "a member of J. P. Morgan & Co., the banking firm in which Mrs. Lindbergh's father, the late Senator Dwight W. Morrow, was a partner until he was appointed Ambassador to Mexico by former President Coolidge."

When Red was laid off in October, he once again moved in with his brother Fred in Brooklyn. During the winter months, he worked as an oil worker for the Norton Company at 53rd Street and East River in New York City. He was re-employed on the *Reynard* in April 1931. In August, the yacht sailed to North Haven, Maine. While there, he met up with a friend of his, Alfred Burke, a chauffeur for the Morrow Family. They attended a dance in the village one night and while there, Alfred introduced Red Johnson to a fellow employee at the Morrow Estate – Betty Gow.

Betty Gow was "…a pretty, dark-haired Glasgow girl, [who] came to the United States…and worked in various homes and hotels in the West as a nursemaid and housemaid before she was recommended…by Elisabeth Morrow, Mrs. Lindbergh's sister, as an ideal attendant and companion for the [Lindbergh's] baby. She is a friend of Miss Morrow's personal maid…. Miss Gow is 26 years old, cheerful, with an undiminishing smile, slender and extremely light on her feet."

Red returned with the *Reynard* to New York in September and in early October he sailed with it up the Harlem River where it was laid up for winter dry-docking at the Consolidated Ship Yard at Morris Heights. Later that month, he began to date Betty Gow on a regular basis. He bought a used green Chrysler Coupe and moved to Englewood, New Jersey, to be near his new girlfriend, with intentions of eventually marrying her. He roomed with a Finn named Heimu Hattu at 41 James Street. Hattu was a part-time police officer at Palisade Inter-State Park during the summer and worked as a laborer there during the winter months. He and Red would occasionally play pool together at the pool hall near Dean and Van Brunt Streets in Englewood. Red also played pool "over in Brooklyn, [at] a poolroom on 5th Avenue and 52nd Street with my brother…and Carl Hillard. Those are about the only ones I ever played pool with…I learned [the game] over there on 5th Avenue…"

There were few people that Red Johnson considered friends. "Betty Gow, for one, and my brother were about my only friends; in a way, we used to 'hit it up' pretty good together. [Also] Carl Hillard, and there is a family by the name of Thompson in Brooklyn; we were quite friendly, the five sisters and a couple of brothers, quite friendly with them…That is about all – I have very few friends."

Red and Betty dated on average three times a week. He visited her at the Morrow estate, taking her to the movies or simply out riding in his Chrysler. They would usually go out alone, but would occasionally double date with another couple – Roland Craver and Edith Monroe. "On one occasion on New Year's Eve, we went to a road house, the Foliage, at Closter and also went skating with them at Bear Mountain Park." From time to time, while out on dates with Betty, Roland and Edith, the conversation would turn to the Morrows, the Lindberghs and, of course, the Lindbergh Baby. But this amounted to nothing more than curiosity and idle chatter.

Red also visited the Lindbergh estate in Hopewell, New Jersey, with Betty on three occasions. The first visit was in November 1931. He took Betty down on her day off because she had never been to the house before that time. While there, they met Ollie and Elsie Whateley, the Lindberghs' butler and cook. "Sometime that day we went all through the house and Mr. and Mrs. Whateley explained to us who would occupy the different rooms, including the baby's room and Colonel Lindbergh's room. On that occasion Mr. Whateley and I walked down to the woods where they had erected several poles for the power lines."

Their second visit to Highfields, as the Lindbergh estate was known, took place on New Year's Day, 1932:

> "Betty had come up to Englewood the previous night when we had gone out [to] the New Year's party and she had to return to Hopewell New Year's Day. She had asked me to drive her there and I had told her I would do so…We arrived shortly before noon and Betty had to go right to her duties…. Mr. Whateley asked me to have lunch there, which I did, and then I stayed in the servants' quarters all that afternoon, had supper there and left the house alone in my car and returned to Englewood."

The last visit to Hopewell was on Valentine's Day, 1932. It was a Sunday afternoon and Betty had the day off work. She suggested that they drive to Hopewell to visit the Whateleys. Arriving around 4:00 in the afternoon, they had tea in the servants' quarters with Ollie and Elsie. They ate dinner between 7:00 and 8:00 that evening and afterwards, the Whateleys, along with Betty and Red, went to the sitting room on the first floor. Around 8:30, Red went out to the garage where he had left his car to add some oil to the engine.

I had the extra oil in a bottle in the rear of the car but as it was cold it took quite a while to put the oil in the car. I think it took me about twenty minutes and I then returned to the house and then went to the second floor toilet in the servants' quarters to wash my hands and then returned to the sitting room to join Betty and the Whateleys.

Betty and Red stayed at Highfields with the Whateleys until 9:45 that evening and then returned to Englewood.

The last time Red Johnson saw Betty Gow was on February 29, 1932. On that night, Betty, Red, Captain Christiansen of the *Reynard* and his wife and four other Morrow servants were playing cards in the servant quarters of the Morrow estate. Before leaving for the night, Red asked to see Betty again the next evening, because he had plans to leave for Hartford, Connecticut on Wednesday morning to visit his brother. Betty agreed to see him.[3]

At 8:30 in the morning of March 1st, Red took the bus to the Dumont, New Jersey, the hometown of Captain Christiansen. He ate breakfast with the Captain and his wife and then helped him simonize his car. The Captain then drove him back to Englewood around 4:00 that afternoon.

Upon his arrival home, Red's landlady – Mrs. Sherman – told him that Betty had called in the morning and requested that he call her back at the Morrow estate when he returned. He went to the local drug store to make the call, but learned that Betty had left for Hopewell to help care for the Lindbergh baby.[4]

Around 6:30 that evening, Red went to a lunch wagon on Grand Avenue in Englewood for a light dinner. He then read the newspaper there until about 7:15. Bored, he went for a ride and parked at Palisade Avenue until 8:00 pm when he decided to visit the Junges. Marguerite Junge was a friend of Betty's and worked as a seamstress at the Morrow estate. When he arrived, she was not home, but her husband, Johannes, was there and welcomed Red into their apartment. Marguerite eventually arrived and told Red "…that Betty Gow had told her she was sorry she had to leave Englewood for Hopewell and that she was not able to keep our appointment for Tuesday night. [She asked] for me to go to Hartford, Connecticut, as I had planned and either write or get in touch with her when I returned."

Red asked Marguerite for the Lindberghs' number and at 8:30 – when the telephone rates were cheaper – he called Betty in Hopewell. Calling from a drug store on Palisade Avenue and Humphrey Street, he spoke to Betty for about five minutes:

> A man I thought was [Ollie Whateley] the butler…answered
> the phone and I asked him if I could speak to Betty Gow…
> [she] then spoke to me on the telephone and after some
> conversation about how she was and what kind of trip she
> had and what time she left Englewood, I then inquired
> about the baby as Mrs. Junge had told me the Lindbergh
> baby was sick and that it was on account of the baby's illness
> that [she] had to go to Hopewell…Betty told me the baby
> seemed much better.

Betty informed Red that she would most likely return to Englewood sometime on Wednesday. He asked if he should still leave for Hartford as he planned or would she like him to wait until they had a chance to see each other again on Wednesday evening. He could then leave Thursday morning.

> Betty asked if my brother expected me. I told her I had
> written [him] that I would be there Wednesday afternoon.
> [She] then said that since my brother expected me I had
> better go to Hartford and not wait to see her. [I should]
> either write or get in touch with her when I get back to
> Englewood [the following Wednesday]…She wished me a
> good trip, told me to drive carefully and to be a good boy.

After receiving Betty's blessing to continue with his travel plans, Red returned to the Junges' apartment and, at about 9:45, took them out for a ride in his car.

> We drove to a confectionery store, next to the Plaza Theater
> in Englewood,[5] and had some ice cream and then drove
> up Palisade Avenue to the Hendrik [sic] Hudson Drive at
> Dykman Ferry, following the Hendrik Hudson along the
> Hudson River to Alpine, where we turned onto the State
> Road No. 9 following that road back to Palisade Avenue, and
> then to the Morrow home where Mrs. Junge left us, arriving
> there about 11:30 pm. I then took Mr. Junge to his house
> and then I went to my house – arriving there about 12:00
> midnight [parking] my car in the rear of the house. Then I
> packed some clothes in a grip and went to bed.

Around 8:00 the next morning, Red went out to a restaurant on Palisade Avenue for breakfast. While there, the waitress showed him the headlines from the New York Daily News announcing that the Lindbergh Baby had been kidnapped the night before. Red ran across the street to a newsstand and bought a copy of the Herald-Tribune, which he took home with him to show Mrs. Sherman, his landlady. "I told her it did not seem possible that the child could have been kidnapped at 8:00 [as printed in the article] as I had spoken to the nurse at 9:00[6]…and didn't hear anything about it at that time."

Leaving his paper with Mrs. Sherman, he prepared to begin his trek to Hartford. Red changed the oil in his car and then retrieved his grip from his upstairs room. On his way out, he left his brother's address and telephone number on a small card with his landlady in case anyone needed to get in touch with him. "I also told Mrs. Sherman I would be back Wednesday or Thursday of the following week. Then, I said good-bye and left in my car for Hartford."

Red Johnson got as far as Fordham Road in The Bronx when John Fernino hailed him from the side of the road, looking for a ride to Bridgeport. Red agreed to take him there, as it was along the route to his brother's in Hartford. Along the ride, conversation naturally turned to the Lindbergh kidnapping.

After a brief stop in Stratford, Connecticut, for lunch, Red dropped his passenger off in Bridgeport and then continued on to his brother John's house in Hartford. He arrived there around 1:00 in the afternoon.

> I stayed at my brother's house from then on and on Friday, March 4, 1932, about 6:00 pm, Captain Sullivan of the West Hartford Connecticut Police came to my brother's home and took me to West Hartford Police Headquarters. I was kept at…[there] and later on Detective Hickey arrived and questioned me about the kidnapping and my whereabouts at the time until 11:00 that [evening]. Then I was taken to the State House in Hartford where I was again questioned by Detective Hickey and State Attorney Alcorn till about 5:00 am Saturday, March 5, 1932, and was placed in jail. About 3:00 PM Saturday, March 5, 1932, I was taken to Detective Hickey's home in West Hartford, Connecticut and about 4:00 PM he drove me in his car to Englewood, New Jersey, Police Headquarters…[I was] questioned there by some officers and stayed there over night, being taken the next morning by Detectives McGrath and Schiable to Police Headquarters, Newark, arriving there around noon.

Red Johnson's fingerprints were taken and forwarded to the Identification Bureau of the United States Bureau of Investigation (the agency that later became known as the FBI) as well as police departments in Norway, Denmark, Sweden, England and Austria. The Bureau of Investigation "…was subsequently advised by these authorities that their records did not reflect any previous criminal record of Johnson."

Surprisingly, the New Jersey State Police announced as early as March 7th that they were not interested in Red Johnson as a suspect, "…and are studiously avoiding any attention to what is going on in Connecticut."

On March 13th, Red Johnson was "…cleared of all suspicion of complicity in the kidnapping by Deputy Chief of Police Brex of Newark…" and was transferred to a jail in Jersey City. Regardless of this exoneration, five days later, Colonel Lindbergh summoned Johnson to his home in Hopewell for a "private" interview. Until now, Lindbergh "…displayed no more interest in the matter than he did in any of the many false alarms which marked the feverish first days of the hunt for the kidnappers." Suddenly, Colonel H. Norman Schwarzkopf of the New Jersey State Police was calling on the Jersey City Police informing them "…the famous aviator wanted to question the former sailor himself."

Red spent the next day at Highfields, returning to the Jersey City jail late on March 20th. No other explanation was ever offered for his transfer to Hopewell by the police.

Red remained in the Jersey City jail for another twenty-two days before he was finally transferred to Ellis Island, being turned over to Immigration Officers John W. Williams and Anthony M. McCabe. In a letter from Acting Newark Police Chief F. E. Brex to the Secretary of Labor, William Doak, Brex noted that "in 28 years as a police officer I cannot recall any subject who had received such a diversified investigation with nothing of an incriminating nature being discovered…When we turned over Johnson to your Immigration Officers simultaneously we exonerated Johnson from any connection whatsoever, directly or indirectly, with the kidnapping of the Lindbergh baby."

Held now on Ellis Island under what was then the largest bail ever imposed upon an immigrant -- $50,000 – forces behind the scenes began to work to ensure that Red was not deported, but allowed to leave the country voluntarily.[7] With the assistance of United States Senators and Congressmen, and other government and police officials (including the Director of the Republican National Committee), it was arranged for "…the warrant of deportation to be cancelled upon verification of [his] departure."

The making of Red's departure voluntary rather than an actual deportation would allow him to return legally to the United States in the future. "My intention is to return legally…. as soon as circumstances permit." On Thursday, July 21, 1932, Red Johnson sailed for Norway upon the S/S Tonsbergfjord. His brother Fred paid for his passage. "I'm looking forward to getting home for a vacation in Norway. After that I might sail around the coast a little with my dad, who owns a freight carrier."

Red Johnson left a very positive impression on the authorities in the United States. A further reading of the Brex letter of May 10th shows just how well liked he was by the authorities in Newark:

> I personally and officially feel that Johnson did not have anything to do with that crime. Johnson impresses me as a fine type of young man, a boy, who, in my opinion, had a very fine bringing up; a perfect gentleman, and an outstanding type of young man.

This was not the case in Hartford, Connecticut. In an interview with the Norwegian-American newspaper, Nordisk Tidende, Red Johnson was asked if the police gave him the third degree: "The police in Newark have treated me in the best of ways, but in Hartford…they were brutal. I was questioned non-stop for hours. The detectives swore and yelled at me in every way, while they kept poking me with their knuckles, here, in the ribs and in the belly."

The treatment was more severe than he admitted to in the interview. According to his daughter, "…In the summer he was naked on the upper part of his body and it was marks [from cuts]…on the front and back as thick as your little finger…" He was also kept in a cell so small he could not sit or lie down – with water dripping down on his head.

The emotional scars Red suffered were just as severe as the physical scars:

> He was [a] cheerful man. And when he was working, he was happy when he was making things because he was very clever with his hands. He was always doing something either for us or for other people. He was enjoying himself, singing and whistling. But then we notice he would get nervous and restless and some few days after he started drinking. Then he drank for about fourteen days. He bought everything that he needed, went to bed, laid in bed for fourteen days and drank. And when that was finished he rose up and started walking around and working again. And that went on all his life.

Red's first stop in Norway in July 1932 was his hometown, Moss. He worked odd jobs while living with his family in the Blekkhuset, or "Ink House." This is a small house located on Nesvegen, a street in northern Jeløya. It got its name because it resembles an old-fashioned ink house or ink well. "It was built in 1912…but my grandparents bought it some years after [circa 1920]…my grandmother and father's oldest sister lived in that house until they both died. After that it was sold."

Once home, Red became re-acquainted with a childhood friend, Randi Olsen. The Olsen and Johansen families were acquainted and Red and Randi dated for a while before he left for America in 1927. Soon after his return to Norway, they were engaged to marry.

Red moved to Oslo, to be near his fiancée. Red's first challenge was finding employment. This was not an easy task for an unskilled "deck-hand" during the worldwide Depression of the 1930s. Randi's mother, Edle Olsen, was a successful fruit and vegetable merchant in Oslo. She "…was a very busy woman. She had two brothers living in America and she visited them seven times during the Second World War. She was very clever at earning money… She bought a lot of things and sold them and got a lot of money…[she] always had opportunity to earn money from nothing…"

Edle Olsen bought Red a truck that he used to transport fruits and vegetables from the markets to her store. Eventually, she set him up with "…a little shop where he sold chocolate and ice cream and hot dogs and such and [he] made a living out of that." This shop was located on Trondheimsveien in the Sinsen section of Oslo.

Even though Randi's mother helped establish Red in business, she was not happy when he married her daughter in November 1934. This was "because what had happened to him [in America], he was not rich, he was not earning money. He was not for her daughter." Red was also being followed. From the summer of 1932, when he arrived home, until sometime in 1934, Red was followed by a mysterious black car:

> There was a car with two people that followed them everywhere. They didn't know who it was, if they were Norwegian or American people. That was a strange thing, to have this car follow them. If they would travel to other parts of the country, always this black car would follow them.

The car always kept at a distance, never interacting with Johnson or his fiancée until one day they went to visit Red's mother.

> On one occasion when he visited…his mother in Moss, this
> car came up and stopped outside the home. In the garden
> was a little girl about the same age as the Lindbergh child,
> with curly, light hair…These people [in the car] came into
> the house and demanded them to take the clothing off the
> child because they believed it may be the Lindbergh child…
> but this was a little girl, so they had to leave [and Red was
> never followed] again.

Red and Randi were married in November 1934 in Oslo where their daughter, Else Marie, was born. They wanted to adopt a little girl named Synnøve. Prior to leaving for America in 1927, Red had a child with another woman out of wedlock. "Her mother died very early…She was often over when I was very little and my mother and father wanted to adopt her, but it was my grandmother who said 'no'. That was my father's mother. [So] she was brought up by her mother's mother."

Red and his family lived for a while with his mother-in-law, later moving to an apartment on Niels Juels Gate that Edle helped them get near Filipstad Harbor. They lived here from 1935 until 1942 when there was a massive explosion of nitroglycerine. The surrounding buildings – including the apartment building where the Johnsons lived – were badly damaged. "All the windows and doors were blown up and furniture and everything was destroyed…. I got so scared I couldn't sleep in the night after that. Because of this, we moved to Moss. [My father] lived in Moss the rest of his life."

The return to Moss had a dramatic effect on Red Johnson and his family. Once again, Red was unemployed and Randi's flower shop became the only source of income. Randi spent the week living and working in Oslo while Red and Else remained behind in Moss. Because Randi was away during the week, it was up to Red to raise their daughter. "He was a very good father for me. He learned me everything…to sew, to cook, to wash…he was clever. Everything I learned as a child I learned from him."

Red Johnson was a very talented and clever man. "He was very fond of children, and children loved him and followed him because he was always to tell them about what to do and how to do it." He was always thinking of ways to do things that were not done before. "He could mend a car, he could build a house, he could make a radio from odds and ends. He built our house all by himself, but he was not a money earner…he wasn't interested in that part of life. He was interested in making things."

Red did, indeed, build their home. When the family returned to Moss, they rented an apartment on Nesvegen, just a short distance north of the Blekkhuset they had lived in earlier. They moved into the apartment around

Christmas 1943. The bottom floor of the house was a grocery store and the second floor was where they had their apartment. Red began building their new house further up the street, completing it around 1947. He built the house with a little help:

> When he built this house for my family, there was an island in the Oslofjord called Bastøy. This was a prison island for young boys – [juvenile delinquents]. Somehow, he managed to go out there and get some of these boys...to help with some heavy things around the house, like lifting beams and putting tiles on the room. And he had several groups of these young boys to help him. They would have a good time. He knew what it was to be in prison.

In the early 1950s, Red did work again. He found a job on a freighter that brought him again to the United States, around 1951. He visited, briefly, with his brothers whom he had not seen since he left the United States in 1932. He did not say much about his visit to America other than that it was nice to meet his brothers and their families again. "And he bought a lot of tools that he couldn't buy in Norway, like electrical carpenter tools and such. And he was so pleased! [He did carpentry] and made furniture...everything."

Red also went to South Georgia for whale hunting. "*He* didn't do whale hunting; he worked as a carpenter on the island. He was there for a year about the early 50s I think it was. It was South Georgia, the English-owned island. But the whale hunters, almost every one of them was from Norway."

Living in Moss was not an easy life for Red and his family. While living in Oslo, he was relatively anonymous. Once he returned to his hometown, however, the anonymity was gone – everyone knew who he was and what had happened to him in America. Once again, the whispering began. And not always just behind his back. Although Red Johnson was exonerated in the United States, the 'good people' of Moss did not believe in him.

> They talked about [the Lindbergh Case], as they liked to think about it in their own way. That was bothering my father a lot because very often they came with things to him and the most that hurt him was that they said 'isn't it strange that you can do [so much], you can live...that you can have what you have because that's the money from the Lindbergh child.' And only a few months before he died was the last time he heard about that.

Even Red's daughter Else was not immune from such harassment. When she was a child, similar things were said to her by children in her neighborhood and school, such as "'Oh, you have a new doll? My father told me where your father got that money from...'" This lasted until she was seventeen and was able to move back to Oslo to attend university.

When Else was about five or six years old, her father tried to prepare her for such verbal attacks. "I could always come home and tell what the people had said and we talked about it. We looked through his [scrapbook] and talked about everything he had experienced. It was so that I had to realize that some people were like this and others weren't."

It was during this time in Moss that Red started his binge drinking, yet another factor in making it difficult for him to hold a job. Red was no longer the happy-go-lucky sailor of the 1920s. While still cheerful and friendly, he had periods when he would become moody and nervous and he suffered from bouts of depression. He had become a rather sarcastic and skeptical person.

Red's wife's family did not like him and his own family was upset with the attention they were receiving because of him. His family "...was all the time wondering what did other people think, what did other people mean... they didn't care to make anything out of my father's situation. They wanted to lay low."

There is also a "quirk" to Norwegian – and Scandinavian – culture that made it difficult for Red Johnson to cope. He had no friends in Norway as an adult. This is because "Norwegians are not easy people...we say that you should not be different from the big lot of people because then you can't get in with people...[Red was not your average person] and he didn't want to be. He had no idea to be like everybody...he wanted to do what he wanted to do and not to follow anybody else. Norwegian people are jealous of people. We have something called Jante Law."

The Jante Law (Janteloven, in Norwegian) is a term given to a characteristic of Scandinavian society. It basically states, "'we are envious of our neighbor's good fortune.'"[8] The "law" comes from Aksel Sandemose's novel, "A Fugitive Crosses His Tracks," in which the fictitious Danish town of Jante lives by its own version of the Ten Commandments. (See appendix). "By means of the Law of Jante people stamp out each other's chances in life" and this ties in nicely with Scandinavia's egalitarian tradition. "In order to live by the law of Jante, one must not only show, but prove one thinks no more of themselves than one thinks of the great and powerful 'we'"

Because of all of the whispering and harassment Red and Else were receiving because of the Jante Law and her father's connection to the Lindbergh case; because of all of the things being said to Else, all of the newspaper clippings about her father in his scrapbook from America, it caused her to decide that she had to make up her own mind about things. "Not as a child, but when I was a young person...I had to make up my mind that either if he had done it or if he hadn't done it, it was the same to me. That couldn't make any difference to me. Because, for me, he was my father and such a nice person [and] that had to be how it was...that is a hard decision to make when you are young. [We were] different from every family around and in many ways it made me an outsider. And one thing I learned in my home was to look at things and understand them and react in the right way and be skeptical. So, I am open to hear things but I make up my own thoughts about them. It is a good thing to have in your life, I think, but it's a hard school to learn it."

Red's wife Randi was not a well woman. She had heart trouble that every now and then would cause her to black out. "My father and I learned how to exercise her in some ways and massage her and shake her to revive her. It was sometimes 20 minutes and sometimes a day that she was laid up and she would have to go to the hospital. So he had that as well [on his mind] all the time." But it was Red, not Randi, who died suddenly in 1962 at the age of 57:

> He was very fit [and] slender...He could do anything with his body at age 7. He could climb, he could crawl, and he could do anything. So that heart attack came very suddenly, it was not expected at all. He was out driving his car in Oslo and he had had some two weeks [prior] one attack and he got some medicine; it wasn't a heart attack, so he was operating his car. He drove it to the curb and stopped the car, opened his medicine and died holding them in his hand. It was good for him, a sudden attack, so he didn't suffer.

Else and her mother had had enough of the Lindbergh Case and all of the gossiping that had contributed to making Red Johnson's life a sad and difficult experience. After his death, they burned his scrapbook, saving the few pictures taken of him in America. A few years later, Randi died. "It's as if she was kept alive by him and his care." Both Randi and Red Johnson were cremated and buried in a shady corner of the Jeløya Cemetery.

The Johnson family -- Red, Randi and Else Marie – were very close. "We had to be close because it was so difficult and it was only the three of us. And I was young [when they died] I was 27. That was tough. And it is strange to have children and not have any grandparents [for them]."

"[My father] was a young person who loved life. He came to America to make himself a fortune and he had a good time, seemed to have a good time before this [Lindbergh] case came up. And by coincidence he gets into this case that turned everything around for him. Such things can happen to everybody. We don't know why they happen to us. I think he could see that and he could live with that. And he was thankful that it ended like it did [with his exoneration] and he was thankful to a lot of persons that had helped him. And he was not bitter, but he had...this drinking and nervousness... something must really be inside him. But then again...he was a young man in America and a lot of things happened and [when] this case came up, he was in the middle of a great big thing...he was in the middle of the thing that was much bigger than anybody could expect anyone to be in. Coming back to Norway, he sort of collapsed, no one had the fuss about him [anymore]. Everything was negative...I compare it to like an actor or a sportsman who succeeded in some very good things and has a lot of publicity and suddenly, bang! it collapses. Because he came home and there was no job, and my mother's family didn't like him and he didn't make any friends. But he was a nice man and he was my father and I loved him."

2. Hauptmann's Car

On March 3, 1931 Bruno Richard Hauptmann left his residence at 1462 Needham Avenue in the Bronx and made his way to the Williamsbridge Motor Inc at 3516 White Planes Avenue. There he met with Victor Montuari, a car salesman, and placed an order for a 1930 Dodge Brothers DD 6 cylinder sedan. "[He] walked in…and stated that he wanted to buy a clean used car [but] they did not have any used ones available at the time." Delivery was scheduled for March 10th and he left a deposit of $27 in a combination of $25 cash and $2 on credit. The remaining $710 would be paid by way of daybook payments.

On March 9th, Hauptmann received word that his car had arrived a day early. The car was dark blue with light blue striping and wire wheels. A spare tire and lube was included in the $737 price. Hauptmann told the salesman "…that he was going to have the spare tire rack removed from the rear of the car and put it on the side and have a trunk put on the rear so that he could carry his tools in it."

After picking up his car, he had it registered with Motor Vehicles, which cost him $13. 50. He was issued tag number 7U 5291. It was customary at that time to issue new tags each time the car registration was renewed so the plates issued in 1931 would be different from the license plates on the car when he was arrested in 1934.

During the summer of 1931 the Hauptmanns, along with their close friend Hans Kloppenburg, drove cross-country to visit Richard's sister Emma in California. Hauptmann made a small trunk for the back of the car that had two drawers to hold clothes, camping equipment and other supplies. The lid folded down to serve as a table for meals eaten while on the road.

Hauptmann had only been driving the new car for about a month when he received his first of two traffic tickets in Jamaica, New York. The first one was issued on April 17, 1931 when he ran a red light. He was convicted and paid a $5 fine. Just a year later, on April 12, 1932, he ran yet another red light and received a ticket. Later that same year, Hauptmann was involved in an automobile accident.

At 2:35 on a rain October 17th, Richard Hauptmann and his wife Anna were riding along 3rd Avenue with Anna's niece Maria and her husband Hans Müller when Alexander Begg "…crossed [the] street against the light. When he saw my car coming, he tried to go back but he slipped and fell just in front of the car." Hauptmann further stated that he was driving about 15 miles per hour when the accident occurred.

Richard Hauptmann agreed to pay $300 in installments to Mr. Begg and the payments began in December 1932. He paid all but $60 of the settlement and in December 1933 Hauptmann wrote a letter to Mrs. Begg claiming that he was unable to pay the full amount because his wife just had a baby and he needed to save as much money as possible. Even so, he eventually paid her $20.

Hauptmann continued to drive his car without incident around the streets of New York. At around 10:00 in the morning on Saturday September 15, 1934 he pulled into the Warner-Quinlan gas station at 127th and Lexington in Manhattan. There he purchased 5 gallons of gas, which came to 98 cents, and he paid for it with a $10 gold certificate.

Walter Lyle, the station manager, said that Hauptmann "…got out of the car and…took out an envelope and took a gold certificate out of it…I looked at it and remarked casually, 'you don't see many of these any more,' and just as casually he said, 'No, I only have about100 left.'"

Concerned that the bank might not accept this now out-of-date currency, Lyle copied down Hauptmann's license number – NY 4U-1341 – on the edge of the bill as Hauptmann got back into his car. Hauptmann left and Lyle turned the $10 over to his assistant, John Lyons, as part of his wages. Lyons took the money to the bank and changed the $10 bill for two fives.

Later, a bank teller noticed that the $10 gold certificate was actually part of the Lindbergh ransom money and called the police. They in turn traced the license number that Lyle had written on the bill back to Hauptmann and on September 19th he was arrested in connection with the Lindbergh kidnapping.

Hauptmann's car was taken to the 30th Precinct of the New York City Police at 152nd Street and Amsterdam Avenue where it was stripped of all upholstering, lining and contents – all of which were taken to the Bureau of Criminal Information on Greenwich Street for examination by police chemists "…for any evidence they might disclose useful to the prosecution."

Some of the upholstery, lining and confiscated contents still exist today in storage at the New Jersey State Police Museum in West Trenton, New Jersey, as does the trunk Hauptmann made for his California trip.

A license plate bearing the 1934 registration NY 4U 1341 turned up on the Internet auction site eBay but its current location is unknown.

Hauptmann's car was transferred to the New Jersey State Police and was stored in the garage in West Trenton. Eventually it was stripped of its hubcaps, cowl lights, door handles and radiator ornaments. In January 1943 Hauptmanns car was turned in for scrap as part of the State of New Jersey's contribution to the war effort.

3. Hans Kloppenburg

Hans Kloppenburg was born on June 30, 1899 in Schleswig-Holstein, Germany, near the city of Hamburg. Tall and slender, he stood six feet two inches tall with grey eyes and thinning hair. He spoke with a thick German accent and was a very distinguished looking gentlemen whom friends dubbed „*der Lange Hans*" ("The Tall Hans") from the song „*Spannenlanger Hansel, nudeldicke Dirn.*"

Hans Kloppenburg and Richard Hauptmann first met in the summer of 1930. They were both working at *Langenbacher*, a cabinetmaker, located on 72nd Street near the East River. After leaving the company, Hans and Richard worked together again on a house "downtown on the Westside…in the twentieth streets somewhere" doing carpentry.

The two men became close friends over the years. "We were like brothers…[Richard was] the best friend I ever had." Hans would visit Richard at his house on most Saturdays and there they would have a "musical evening" where they would sing and play music: Richard on the mandolin and Hans on the guitar and mandolin. [9]

When the Hauptmanns drove cross-country in July 1931 to visit Richard's sister Emma in California, Hans Kloppenburg went along. He, too, had a sister in California and this trip afforded him not only an opportunity to visit her but also to see the country and spend time with his closest friends. As often happens on such trips there was tension and when they returned in October Hans didn't see the Hauptmanns again for a couple of months. When asked about this, he stated, "we had not a little argument…I didn't go to him and he didn't come to me…While we were on the trip his wife was thick-headed and didn't talk to me on the way back…We had souvenirs and I didn't say something to him, but I had a lot of post cards and I missed some and I don't know if they took some of mine." Richard, however, went to Hans' apartment in January to visit him and the two of them rekindled their friendship.

Shortly after their return from California, Hans took a job working out of his apartment making display stands for a man called Rieger. He was paid 50 cents per stand, but it was not steady work. "He give me an order and I don't work for another couple of days."

On December 2, 1933 Richard Hauptmann threw a bon voyage party for his business partner, Isidor Fisch. Fisch was sailing for Germany to visit family in Leipzig. Although Hans attended the party, he did not include himself as one of his friends. He felt that Fisch was "a sneaky, foxy sort of guy. You never knew where you were with him."

After Richard Hauptmann was arrested spending Lindbergh ransom money, he claimed that Isidor Fisch had given it to him. He said that prior to Fisch leaving for Germany, Fisch gave him a shoebox to hold until his return. Fisch, who suffered from tuberculosis, died while in Germany. Allegedly, Hauptmann opened the box, found money inside and began to spend it. This shoebox, Richard said, was given to him the night of the farewell party. Hans Kloppenburg was the only other person who claimed to have seen the box. He said that when Fisch arrived, "he brought a package wrapped in paper and tied with string…and [it] looked like a shoebox." He said that he and Richard went into another room with the box but that they closed the door so he could not see what they were doing with it.

Soon after Hauptmann's arrest, the New York police also arrested Kloppenburg. The police interrogated him about Hauptmann and their dealings together. They also took samples of his handwriting for comparison with that of the ransom notes. Finding no connection between Hans Kloppenburg and the Lindbergh Kidnapping, he was released, but was called as a defense witness.

When it came time to testify at the Grand Jury hearing in the Bronx, the prosecution did not want Hans to testify in support of Hauptmann's claim that Isidor Fisch had given him the ransom money in the shoebox. Hans claimed that New York detectives tried to prevent his testimony by means of threats and intimidation:

> The detectives or the DA's men took me into a private room
> and started talking about what electricity does to the body, all
> the terrible things that happen when a man is electrocuted.
> They were trying to scare me with the electric chair so that
> I wouldn't testify. And they threatened to put me in prison.
> But I testified anyway.

A few days before he was to testify at Hauptmann's trial in Flemington, New Jersey Attorney General David Wilentz summoned Kloppenburg to his hotel suite at the Hotel Hildebrecht in Trenton. Wilentz told him, "'if you say on the witness chair that you [saw] Fisch come in with the shoebox, you'll be arrested right away'. I was very surprised that he said that. I told him, 'but I seen it! I seen him come in the house with the shoebox. It's the truth!' And he said if I talk about the shoebox, I'm going to be in a lot of trouble. Then…the day before I testified, there was a story in the newspapers that the police were about to arrest a second man in the kidnapping. That was *me* they were talking about! They were trying to scare me so I would shut up. And I was scared. So when I testified, I never called it a shoebox. I described it…but I never used the word."

After his best friend's conviction and execution, Hans Kloppenburg realized he would have to move forward and get on with his life. He continued to work with wood, spending the rest of his life as a self-employed carpenter and cabinetmaker. He eventually moved away from the Bronx, and settled in the Jackson Township area of New Jersey. A religious man, he attended the Immanuel Lutheran Church in nearby Lakewood. He continued singing and was a life member of the Lakewood Männerchor (the Lakewood Men's Choir), even serving as president at one time. Hans remained active throughout his life and was a member of the Jackson Township Senior Citizen's Club.

Hans married and in May 1982 his wife Lina died. Seven years later, on Tuesday, January 3, 1989, Hans Kloppenburg passed away. A sister in Germany, his daughter Gladys, a granddaughter and three great-grandchildren survived him. Hans lived a full and active life and was 89 years old when he died.

4. Attorney General David Wilentz

David Theodore Wilentz was born in *Dwinsk*, Latvia, on December 21, 1894. He immigrated to the United States with his parents around 1900 and settled in Perth Amboy, New Jersey. He became a naturalized citizen and attended public schools, graduating from Perth Amboy High School in 1912. He then took a job at the Perth Amboy Evening News and managed the local basketball team while attending New York Law School in the evenings.

When the United States entered the First World War in 1917, David Wilentz enlisted in the army as a Private and rose to the rank of Lieutenant. After returning from his military service, he was admitted to the New Jersey Bar in 1919. That same year he founded the law firm *Wilentz, Goldman and Spitzer* in neighboring Woodbridge, New Jersey.

In 1928, Wilentz was appointed the City Attorney of Perth Amboy. Later that year he was elected chairman of the Middlesex County Democratic Party and was responsible for helping to sweep the Republicans out of office in that county after a ten-year monopoly.

Although he had never tried a criminal case, on February 5, 1934 – at the urging of Jersey City mayor and political boss Frank Hague – Governor A. Harry Moore appointed Wilentz New Jersey's 36th Attorney General. The following year, Wilentz tried his first criminal case – one that garnered him worldwide fame. On January 2, 1935 the opening gavel sounded on the trial of Bruno Richard Hauptmann for the kidnapping and murder of Charles Lindbergh, Jr.:

During the trial…the prosecutor's demeanor attracted instant attention. A short, wiry man, Mr. Wilentz dressed nattily and spoke with a sharp, satirical tongue that he had used to good advantage in political caucuses. Outside the courthouse, cameras focused on his sassafras-colored felt hat.

During the Hauptmann trial, Wilentz tended to treat witnesses under cross examination in a way that some modern "trail watchers" consider bullying while others consider it simply passionate. Joseph Mitchell, a reporter for the *World-Telegram* reported in his January 30, 1935 article that Wilentz would begin his questioning of a witness by reading from a typed document that he would hold in his hands. Before he would finish the question, he would end up "…shaking it violently beneath the nose of the witness. He has violent courtroom mannerisms. When he grabs the kidnap ladder, he grabs it vigorously, picking it up with one hand and slamming it down on the floor in front of the jury box with a bang."

Mitchell's article did, however, point out a lighter side to the Attorney General's character. Apparently Wilentz was rather "…fond of the courtroom pointer, a long wooden pole similar to a billiard cue…He holds the pointer across his lap when he is sitting. Sometimes on his feet, he cups his palms over the handle of the pointer and rests his chin on his knuckles. During a recess today he gratified a desire he has repressed since the trial began. He stretched out his right hand and tried to balance the up righted pointer on his index finger. He did not succeed."

David Wilentz served as Attorney General until 1944. In 1950, he helped found the National Democratic Club of New Jersey. Very active in Democratic politics, and a close advisor to each New Jersey governor the Democrats elected, by 1960 he was a member of the Democratic National Committee and had been a delegate to every Democratic National Convention since 1940.

In 1919, David Wilentz married Lena Goldman. They had three children, Warren, Robert and Norma. The family never moved from Perth Amboy, the town he called home since his emigration from Latvia. They did maintain a summer home at Long Branch, New Jersey, and it was there that he died peacefully on July 6, 1988 at age 93. Never having retired from his law practice, he was working in his office just two days before he passed away. His wife and children, eight grandchildren and five great-grandchildren survived him.

Mrs. Wilentz died in June 1991 and his son Robert, who was the Chief Justice of the New Jersey Supreme Court for seventeen years, died in 1996. Attorney General Wilentz is buried at the Beth Israel Memorial Park in Woodbridge, New Jersey.

5. Robert Peacock

Assistant Attorney General Robert Peacock was born on August 19, 1883 in Conshohocken, Pennsylvania and his family moved to Florence, New Jersey when he was a young child. He and his wife and children spent many years at their summer home in Atlantic City until 1926 when they moved to their permanent home in Brigantine.

Robert Peacock followed a rather unorthodox road to the state bar and the Attorney General's office. He dropped out of school at age 12 when he had completed the 8th grade. Later, he would attend Rider Business College in Trenton where he gained fame as a star track athlete and, for ten years, he played in the Burlington County Baseball League.

After leaving school to find work, he took a position at the Florence Thread Company while studying stenography at night. This paid off because in 1905 he was given a job as secretary to State Assembly Speaker Samuel K. Robbins. While working for Speaker Robbins, Peacock studied law and, in 1906 he was hired to work in the Mt. Holly office of Prosecutor Samuel A. Atkinson. After passing the state bar exam in 1910, Atkinson made him an assistant prosecutor.

In 1913 Peacock was elected to the State Assembly from Burlington County and, in 1915 was given the post of County Solicitor for the Board of Freeholders, a position he held for a decade. Then, in 1927 he was appointed police recorder for the town of Brigantine, New Jersey.

In 1928 he caught the attention of Attorney General William A. Stevens who appointed Peacock as a special prosecutor and Assistant Attorney General. He did well in this position and in 1933 the new Attorney General, David T. Wilentz, re-appointed Peacock as his Assistant.

In 1934, Assistant Attorney General Peacock was assigned to help prepare the State's case against Bruno Richard Hauptmann. "Over a period of six and a half months, Peacock checked the statements of 310 witnesses, and examined 315 documents and exhibits as well as having prepared the entire case and having assisted at the trial.

Peacock had an exemplary record during his legal career, both as a prosecutor and as a trial lawyer. He was the defense counsel in over thirty murder cases and out of all that, only one man was given the death penalty. Ironically, as the prosecutor in twenty trials he never lost a case.

The difficult road that Peacock followed to attain his successful law career had a lasting impact on him. Never forgetting from where he came, "he always had deep sympathy for persons who needed legal assistance but could not afford it, and many a client was served capably without it costing a fee."

Robert Peacock died after a brief illness in Brigantine, New Jersey when he was 72 years old.

6. Jafsie

One of the most enigmatic and complex players in the Lindbergh Kidnapping Case was Dr. John F. Condon. Using the codename *Jafsie* (taken from his initials J-F-C), Condon served as the intermediary between the kidnapper(s) and the Lindbergh family – to the exclusion of the police.

The simplest biographical sketch of Condon and his involvement in the case could fill a book. What follows here, then, is not an attempt to discuss his role in detail nor an attempt to gloss over and short change Condon's importance to the case. Rather, it is meant to show that there was more to Condon's life – much more – than simply what occurred during the "Lindbergh Years." [10]

John Francis Condon was born on June 1, 1860 in the Bronx – a borough of New York that he later declared "the most beautiful borough in the world." His father, John Condon, Sr., emigrated from Ireland in 1848 at age 27. His mother, Ellen Conlon, was born in Albany, New York in 1832. John F. Condon, Jr. was one of eight children.

Condon attended high school at PS 61, graduating as Valedictorian in 1877. He continued on to college, receiving in 1882 his Bachelor's degree at City College of New York. He earned a second Bachelor's degree at St. John's College, although the year of graduation is unknown. He earned his Master's degree at Fordham University in 1902 and a Ph. D in Pedagogy in 1904 at New York University.

From 1882 to 1883 he worked for Western Union where Condon learned telegraphy. In November 1883 he took the City Superintendent's examination for teachers. Having passed, he spent the rest of his life teaching and serving as both vice principal and principal in various schools in the Bronx Public School System. At one point he claimed that in eighteen years he never missed a day of teaching and never reported or dismissed a single child for disorderly conduct in class.

Condon loved to write poems and letters to the editor, especially the editors of the *North Side News* and the *Bronx Home News*, both local Bronx newspapers, signing them with a clever *nom de plume* such as "P. A. Triot" (for *Patriot*) or "L. O. Nestar" (for *Lone Star*). It was this kind of play on words that led him to create his most famous moniker, *Jafsie*.

Condon also published three books: *A Chronological Table of the Battles of the Civil War in Verse* (1888); *Mnemonics: Spelling, Grammar, Arithmetic, Business Calculation, College Exams, Civil Service Questions* (1893); and *Condon's Quick Calculation* (1915). [11]

When Condon was not busy writing or teaching, he was involved with sports. Known as the "Tremont Peach", he was voted best all-around baseball player in the Bronx while in high school and college. Playing several years on the Bronx *Emeralds* baseball team, he also umpired many games in the Bronx earning the title "Old American Eagle Eye." He also managed *The Suburban Club* baseball team for five years. Their clubhouse was on the corner of Park Avenue and 176th Street and they played their games at Crotona Park, at East Tremont and Arthur Avenues in the Bronx.

Condon won many awards for his involvement in sports including the *James Godwin Medal* for best all-around athlete at New York College, the *autographed flag* of the American Athletic Club All-Around Championship Athlete; the *Byrnes' Medal* for being champion sprinter of New York; sixty gold medals for various athletic contests and a gold watch from the *Baseball Friends of the Bronx World* that was presented to him on September 25, 1902 by Commissioner Henry Bruckner.

In addition to his writing, teaching and athletic legacy, John Condon was an all around hero. According to an FBI review of Condon's scrapbooks, there are at least six documented instances of his lifesaving actions:

In February 1886, Condon saved the life of Henry Schaeffer who had fallen through the ice at Zeltner's Lake in the Bronx. An Act of Congress awarded him a gold lifesaving medal on June 20, 1894 "in testimony of heroic deeds in saving life from the perils of the sea…for rescuing a boy from drowning, February 1886." [12]

Two years later, in 1888 Commissioner of Education DeBavaise presented a pair of ice skates to Condon on behalf of the City of New York for saving the life of a person who fell through the ice in the 110th Street Lake in Central Park. A few years later, sometime around the turn of the century, 9-year-old Walter Hoy was skating in Crotona Park and fell into Crotona Lake. Fortunately for him Condon was there and saved him from drowning.

In 1903 Condon saved 19-year-old David Lickefberg when he broke through the ice on Van Cortlandt Lake. Prior to this, Condon had jumped from Doyles Pier at Staten Island to save a boy after he sank beneath the surface for a third time. It was stated in a newspaper article that "this was the fourth life [Condon] has saved."

It was during a respite from his lifesaving heroics that in 1894 Doctor Condon married fellow teacher Myra Brown of Harlem. They had three children; John, Lawrence and Myra.

The Condons lived at various addresses in New York City, finally settling at 2974 Decatur Avenue, the address made famous in the Lindbergh Case. Condon also maintained a small "summer home" on City Island, a small island off the coast of the Bronx. Interviews with old time residents of the island revealed that they did not know John Condon was married with a family on the mainland as he was only seen on the island with his young secretary, Jennie Barton.

Condon taught for 46 years – from January 2, 1884 to June 1, 1930 – when he applied for retirement "…which is the law. I didn't want to take a penny from the City I wasn't entitled to." He was asked, however, to remain for another two years, finally retiring in 1932.

Having invested in real estate, Doctor Condon "…thought it might be wise to learn how to protect it, so I went down to the examination at the Federal Building and passed the examination as realtor." He opened his own real estate office on City Island at 313 City Island Avenue in partnership with his friend and alleged "bodyguard" Al Reich.

As stated earlier, it is not within the scope of this report to discuss Condon's involvement in the Lindbergh Case in great detail. Condon never told the same story twice, so even his reasons for getting involved in the case are cloudy. There is so much confusion, contradiction and deception that even the basic facts surrounding Condon's actions as relating to the case are questionable. What is known is that on March 7, 1932 he wrote a lengthy letter to the editor in which he offered his services to the unknown kidnapper(s) of the Lindbergh baby as a go-between. This article was published in the Bronx Home News the following day. The very next day, March 9th, Condon received a reply from the kidnapper(s) accepting him as intermediary. He passed along a note that was enclosed with his letter to Colonel Lindbergh stating the same and on March 10th Lindbergh authorized Condon to act as his official representative.

Following instructions in the letter he had received, Condon placed an advertisement in the personals section of the newspaper on March 11th.

"Money is Ready – Jafsie" became the first of several such advertisements, which are now commonly referred to as *Jafsie ads*. It was in this way that the kidnapper(s) and the Lindberghs communicated – an advertisement would be placed in the newspaper and a ransom note with further instructions would answer that.

Eventually, Doctor Condon was instructed by the kidnapper(s) to meet their representative on March 12th at Woodlawn Cemetery in the Bronx. Here, he allegedly met with a member of the kidnap gang who became known as *Cemetery John*. Condon claimed to have sat on a bench with him negotiating for over an hour.

A second meeting was arranged for April 2nd at St. Raymond's Cemetery, also in the Bronx. Here, Condon met once again with *Cemetery John* and allegedly paid him the $50,000 ransom. He demanded a receipt for the money, which was given to him in the form of what became the 15th and final ransom note. This note stated that Lindbergh's son could be found on a boat called "Nelly" off the coast of Elizabeth Island in New England. The boat was never found, and a month later, on May 12th, a truck driver named William Allen stumbled upon the remains of Charles Lindbergh, Jr. in the woods, just five miles from the Lindbergh estate.

John Condon continued to "work" on the Lindbergh case over the next two years, reviewing rogues galleries, for example, in an attempt to identify the mysterious *Cemetery John*. His big chance came in September 1934 when Bruno Richard Hauptmann was arrested. Brought in to the police station to witness a line-up that included Hauptmann, Condon refused to positively identify him as the man he met in the Bronx cemeteries. It was not until he was on the witness stand in Flemington, New Jersey, that he dramatically proclaimed that *Cemetery John* was Bruno Richard Hauptmann.

The police at one time suspected Condon as being somehow involved with the Lindbergh kidnapping or at least the ransom extortion. Even though the police could never link him directly to the crime, many researchers of the case today continue to look askance at him and theorize as to his actual role and possible involvement.

The egotistical and grandstanding Jafsie valued the "friendship" he came to believe developed between him and his hero, Charles Lindbergh. For many years after the case was closed he continued to write letters not only to Lindbergh but also to Lindbergh's confidant and aide, Colonel Henry Breckinridge, with whom Condon had worked closely during the investigation. He even went as far as to meet with Lindbergh – in front of cameras, of course – at an America First rally in 1940.

In November 1944, Condon fell ill and was confined to his Decatur Avenue home for several weeks. A nurse was in constant attendance and his doctor visited daily. Finally, on January 2, 1945 – the 10th anniversary of the opening of the trial that brought him international fame and recognition – John Condon died peacefully from pneumonia. He was 84 years old.

Condon's funeral was held on January 4th in the Bronx with a Requiem Mass at St. Philip Neri Church on 205th Street and the Grand Concourse. He was buried in Gate of Heaven Cemetery in Valhalla, New York.

7. Hans and Maria Müller

Maria Dieterle was the daughter of Anna Hauptmann's sister, Bertha. She was born on April 11, 1908 in Mrs. Hauptmann's hometown of *Markgröningen*, in the state of Baden-Württemberg, Germany. She immigrated to the United States in November 1925.

Maria married Hans Müller. Hans was born in Germany on February 19, 1905 and sailed to the United States on the *Westphalia* in 1924. He entered the country illegally after he jumped ship. Hans had a relative living in the Bronx. Gustave Peterson, whose sister had been married to Hans' brother in Germany, owned a boatyard at Classon Point, New York from around 1923 to 1930. Hans came to the boatyard around August 1926 and stayed with Peterson until the spring of 1927. "Müller worked for him doing odd jobs around the boatyard."

In 1927, Müller bought a motor launch for $15 from one of Peterson's customers, but he failed to pay for it. Peterson, not wanting to offend one of his customers, argued with Hans about making payment. Müller apparently refused, so Peterson docked his pay $15 "...and gave it to the party who Müller owed it to. Müller left his employ at this time and sued him for the $15." Peterson had not seen Hans since then.

Sometime around 1928, Hans Müller met Richard Hauptmann. While history does not record the circumstances of how they met, one theory is that they met on City Island, New York. While there is a notation on one of Hauptmann's memo books of one *"Capt. H. Mueller, NY, Marquita c/o Harlem Yacht Club, City Island, NY,"* the Yacht Club denied ever having had any contact with either man. It is possible that Hans used the rank and the club's name to brag.

Investigation into the *Marquita* led the police to Johnson's Boat Yard where they learned that it was a 50-foot sail boat that had the kiel and mast cut down in order to turn it into a party boat. The original owner, Henry Reimers, sold the boat at auction. Hans Müller was a caretaker of the boat and passed himself off to others as its captain.

Henry Reimers told the police that he had purchased the boat from Frank Lewinski and his son Alfred in May 1925. After pestering the Lewinskis for work, they recommended Hans Müller for the job of caretaker on the boat. "Müller did not have any knowledge of navigation and was not permitted to operate the boat." He was employed in 1928 or 1929 and was paid in cash. He went along with Reimers when he sailed to Port Washington, Hempstead Harbor, Glen Cove and "other points in that direction."

It was probably through Hauptmann that Hans met Maria Dieterle, whom he married in 1929. A year later, on November 15, 1930, their only child, a little girl they named Ruth, was born. When Maria would visit her aunt and uncle without Hans, Richard would usually drive her "because it was rather difficult with the baby. She was small then. I went when they called in the car. That was maybe once a month or so."

The Müllers eventually made their home in an apartment on University Avenue in the Bronx while Hans worked at *The Little Hollywood* on East 86th Street. In 1931 he took a job working for Gerhardt Rush at 200 East 86th Street; however he lost this job on February 18, 1932.

Easter came early in 1932, falling on March 27th. The Hauptmanns stopped by the Müllers' apartment for a holiday visit while on their way to Brooklyn and brought two little dresses for Ruth. Hans and Maria had very little cash at this point but they tried to hide this from their aunt and uncle. "[My aunt] did not feel so well and I did not want to tell her straight about how bad off we really were."

Unable to make ends meet, they eventually had to give up their apartment. In early April, the Müllers put their belongings in storage and moved in with Maria's friends for four weeks. Then, on May 1, 1932 they moved into their next apartment on East 159th Street.

Hans was unemployed until sometime in the middle of March 1932 when he finally found work as a waiter at the *York Bar & Grill* at 173 E. 86th Street. It was a new establishment that opened its doors for the first time around March 27th or 30th. Hans took Mondays off, but he had no time off for the first fourteen days that he worked there, and his first day off was his wife's birthday on April 11th. "I had to argue to get that day off. I had to speak to the boss."

The bar employed two waiters and two waitresses. When it first opened, he worked the 7:00 pm to 7:00 am shift for the first two weeks. Later, in

1933, one man would work from lunch until 9:00 in the evening and another from 5:00 pm until 2:00 am. They would exchange shifts every third week. Sometimes they would "split lunch" and would work from noon until 2:30 and then again from 4:45 to 9:00 in the evening. When Hans did this he would "go with the other boys to the park."

On November 3, 1933 Richard and Anna's son was born at the Misericordia Hospital on 86th Street. Maria, the baby's godmother, suggested that the Hauptmanns name their baby *Manfred*. Hans and Maria visited Anna and Manfred at the hospital. "I believe it was the first Monday I was off after the baby was born…[we went] at 2:00, me and my wife, after we have lunch."

When Mrs. Hauptmann was released from the hospital, Maria would visit her four or five times a week to help with the baby and to do the cooking and cleaning. Taking a streetcar, she would arrive around noon and stay until 9:00 or 9:30, when Richard would drive her home.

Hans and Maria moved once again, this time to 2701 Marion Avenue, in spring 1934. "The reasons for Müller moving out of [the] apartment was given as having some argument with the janitor," Mr. Ferdinand Profitlich. He was interviewed and stated that "the Müllers had a party in their apartment and he had received complains from other tenants about the noise. He went up to Müller's apartment and asked them to quiet down, but instead Müller became abusive…[Profitlich] was forced to call a Policeman who ordered the Müllers to quiet down…Müller then came down to [Profitlich's] apartment and invited him out to settle the matter, but he did not pay any attention and Müller moved out of the apartment shortly after."

The Müllers continued to visit the Hauptmanns about once every two weeks, usually staying until 9:00 or 10:00 in the evenings and Richard would always drive them home again. In 1934 Hans stated that he would see Richard about once a week, "because he brought eggs to us once a week from Mr. Blanks' farm, [usually] on Wednesdays. And when there was a Sunday we want to go to Hunters Island, he would come."

1934 was going to prove to be a difficult year for the Müllers. It started with Maria needing surgery in January 1934. Dr. Lewis Sunshine of 9 Gramercy Park performed it and it cost the Müllers $100, approximately $1,540 in 2007 dollars. Everything seemed to be going well for the Müllers' after this. Hans began a new job as a waiter at Schwartz's Restaurant at 183 Broadway and in February or March Richard gave them a nice Radiola. This was a Brunswick-Radiola Super Heterdyne that was a combination radio and victrola. The radio was removed and "remodeled into a sewing cabinet [and the] victrola [was] still intact."

Just a few months later their world would be turned upside down. Back in March 1932 when the news of the Lindbergh baby's kidnapping was broadcast all over the airwaves and newspapers, Hans came home from work and told Maria about the news. "We thought it was terrible. I sat down and cried and thought it was awful to happen." Little did she know then that on September 19, 1934 her uncle would be arrested for that very crime.

Hearing that her uncle had been arrested, she made her way to the Hauptmann residence to take care of Manfred while Mrs. Hauptmann went down to the police station. She arrived at about 5:30 in the afternoon. "I was up there the day they took [my uncle] away...It was after 5:00 because I was in the park...I guess it was half past five...That was on a Wednesday...I stayed there [with Manfred and Ruth]...until Friday morning."

Hans also made his way to the Hauptmanns' house earlier in the day. He was allowed to speak with Anna Hauptmann and they held their conversation in German. New Jersey State Police Detective Sergeant Eugene Haussling, who was fluent in German, overheard the conversation but stated, "nothing of interest was spoken." Hans was then interrogated as to his background and then he joined Mrs. Hauptmann at the police station. At the station, they sat together drinking tea but were not allowed to speak to one another.

At 6:30 in the morning on Friday, September 21st, Hans and Mrs. Hauptmann returned to her home. Because the police, while searching for evidence, had ransacked the house, it was recommended that Mrs. Hauptmann go to the Müllers' apartment to rest. While she and Maria were gathering Anna's belongings, Hans suddenly suffered an epileptic fit and fell to the floor unconscious. Maria hollered from the upstairs window for help and FBI Agents Kavanaugh and Breed ran upstairs accompanied by two policemen. They found Hans lying on the floor in the hall, just outside of the bathroom, "frothing at the mouth and...unconscious."

They quickly administered first aid and after about five minutes, Hans came around and they helped him into bed. One of the policemen called the City Hospital at Fordham and they sent an ambulance and a physician, both arriving around 8:15 that morning.

The doctor examined Hans and said that he had, indeed, suffered a seizure and that he dislocated his shoulder when he fell. The doctor set it for him and advised him "...no hospitalization was necessary but that he should be sure to keep [his arm] in a sling for...two to three days."

After Hans had rested a while, they left for Marion Avenue. When Mrs. Hauptmann and the Müllers finally arrived at their apartment with Ruth and Manfred in tow, "the name of Hans Müller was removed from the mailbox, as well as his apartment bell button, and the [building] superintendent was notified not to furnish information to anyone that Müller lived there."

Only Maria Müller was called to testify at her uncle's trial the following year. She was asked extensively about when she visited the Hauptmanns and served as one of Richard's alibi witnesses for the night of November 26, 1933. That was his birthday and also the day he allegedly passed a ransom bill to Cecilia Barr at the Loew's Sheridan Theatre. Maria testified that Hauptmann was home that evening and that she had been at the Hauptmann's apartment for coffee and cake. She said that he had even driven her home that night, as he usually did when she visited.

Very little is known of Hans and Maria's life after their uncle's conviction and execution. Hans continued to work as a waiter and later as a maitre 'd. Although no official record has yet been found, according to friends of his it is believed that he served in the United States military during World War II. Because he refused to fight against the Germans, he was sent to the Dakotas and served his time there. He returned to New York after the war.

Ruth Müller grew up and married Verne Hilt. Verne's job took him to Mobile, Alabama, and Hans and Maria moved there shortly thereafter. They remained in Mobile for the rest of their lives, helping to raise their three grandchildren.

Hans Müller died in February 1986 and Maria died on March 24, 1999. They are buried in Mobile Memorial Gardens in Tillmans Corner near Mobile, Alabama. Their daughter Ruth died on August 6, 2006.

8. *Highfields*

Shortly after they were married, the Lindberghs began to look for a secluded area where they could build their first home together. Anne gave birth to their first child, Charles Lindbergh, Jr., in June 1930. Later that summer, Lindbergh found 425 acres of land for sale near Princeton, New Jersey in the Sourland Mountains. In September, Anne excitedly wrote to her mother-in-law that, "we have bought that hill with the brook and the fields and the woods of old oaks! It is 19 minutes from Princeton and faces the prevailing breeze and a nice rolling view."

Chester Aldrich, the architect who designed Anne Lindbergh's parents house in Englewood, was hired to design the Lindberghs' new house. Although the house they built was located in Hunterdon County's town of East Amwell, the Lindberghs always referred to the house as the "Hopewell House" and it was not until 1933 that the "Hopewell House" received the name *Highfields*.

While waiting for the construction to be completed, the Lindbergh rented an old farmhouse on 90 acres in nearby Lawrence Township. Known as *White Cloud Farm* it still stands today on Cold Soil Road. They would spend the occasional weekend here; the rest of the time Olly and Elsie Whateley – the butler and maid – served as caretakers, a role they would continue at the Hopewell House.

By March 1931 the quarter-mile long driveway to the Hopewell house was in place and the "digging for the foundations started." The Matthews Construction Company of Princeton supplied the majority of laborers for the project and the Lindberghs were able to spend their first night in the house on Halloween Night, 1931.[13]

The house is a two-and-a-half story stone structure of mixed architectural style – French Tudor Revival and English Tudor Revival. The "exterior walls are of heavy rubble stone construction, utilizing feldspar/granite quarried locally" and finished with a white stucco surface. The steep gabled roof is 1-inch slate and was contoured to resemble the Atlantic Ocean as seen by Lindbergh from the air during his famous transatlantic flight in 1927.

According to A. Scott Berg, Lindbergh's official biographer,

> The whitewashed fieldstone house with its thick slate roof had two wings running perpendicular to and projecting slightly in front of the central section. Through the front hall, one entered the living room, paneled in dark wood. To the left were a library with a dark stone fireplace and a guest room; to the right were the dining room and kitchen, which led to servants' quarters and the large [three-car] garage. Upstairs were the master bedroom, three guest rooms, and, in the back corner farthest from the entrance, the nursery. Pretty blue [Delft] tiles decorated its fireplace; and a table, chair, and crib were already in place. The house had built-in closets and shelves and four bathrooms. There was enough architectural detail to make it attractive without being fancy. The electricity, plumbing, heating, and air conditioning in the house were all top-of-the-line, bringing its total coast to almost $80,000. For all that, none of the rooms had the spaciousness that the towering exterior suggested.

There are a total of 23 rooms, 6 fireplaces, 5 bathrooms and 34 closets in the house. The basement contains a boiler room, storeroom, laundry and workshop. The floors are made of reinforced concrete and the stone walls are 28 inches thick. In 1932, the library "…boasted a huge globe in a beautiful wooden frame. The shelves were not completely filled with books as yet and the rest of the rooms were as yet sparsely furnished." [14]

By March 1932, when the majority of the construction on the house itself was complete, the Lindberghs were spending most weekends at the Hopewell House. Charles, Anne and the baby would arrive on Saturday and stay until either Sunday afternoon or Monday when they would return to the Morrow Estate in Englewood. Anne liked to use these weekend getaways as an opportunity to bond with her baby – by now a toddler who had begun to call his nanny, Betty Gow, "mommy" instead of Anne. It was because of a break in this routine – the family had stayed an extra two nights at the Hopewell House – that led to one of the biggest controversies of the

Lindbergh Case: how did the kidnapper(s) know the family would be in residence at the Hopewell House on a Tuesday night?

After the kidnapping, the Hopewell House began to lose its appeal for Anne. "…There is no use living in the crime element of this any longer, that is what it is at Hopewell now. Constant reconstruction of the crime. I want to dwell on the boy's happy life, not on the crime that ended it."

Anne went on to write, "I feel as if I would like to get away from… Hopewell for a while (thoughtI have grown to love the place strangely in these last months)…C[harles] and I talk about the house at Hopewell and our wanting 'to start all over again.'"

Anne tried to spend as much time as she could in Englewood with her family. On June 26, 1932 she and Charles returned, with Betty Gow, to the Hopewell House and she wrote about it in her diary:

> The house gleams white and fresh…It is cool and peaceful, a home once again – no sign of the case…Then the burnt marks on the stairs of the baby's fingerprints where the men had tried to bring them out chemically…The baby's room was still and peaceful, the big French window wide open, just the same secure intimate room it was in that other world…I don't believe I can ever live in this house in freedom and sanity. That window, that side of the house, the approaches – I shall always be trying to know just what happened in terror and curiosity and misery.

During the summer of 1932, "…the Lindberghs' arranged for Olly and Elsie to go home to England for a six-week respite and needed someone reliable to stay in the house." Arthur Springer, Dwight Morrow's private secretary and, after his death, head of the household staff at the Englewood Estate, "suggested that his brother George and wife Irene take on the job." After speaking with Charles Lindbergh several times on the telephone and eventually meeting with him in person at the Morrow home, George Springer "…received *carte blanche* as to the house and the use of the car – a brand new Model A Ford."

Lindbergh hand wrote directions from Englewood to East Amwell for the Springers and they moved in for the summer with their daughter. "My father cooked for us all including the [State] Troopers; one Trooper stayed in the house with us every night…the [other] Troopers set up headquarters in a farmhouse at the end of the drive where they stopped and questioned all the drivers and passengers of the…cars that were filled with curiosity seekers."

In early August 1932 Charles Lindbergh began discussing with his mother-in-law, Elizabeth Morrow, the idea of turning the Hopewell House into a children's home. Anne was very much in favor of the idea. "It seems to me a very good solution. It satisfies something in me – 'to make it up to the boy,' to make it up to children, anyway, to make good out of evil, if that is possible…Normal use of that place does not seem possible for us or for anyone else (I should dislike any other family using it carelessly, rudely)."

By June 1933 the Lindberghs had "moved out of Hopewell; everything is packed. We are giving the place to a Corporation of Trustees – only five so far – Col. Henry [Breckinridge], Mr. Lovejoy, head of the Children's Aid Society, Abraham Flexner [Director of the Institute for Advanced Studies in Princeton], and C[harles] and I. Mother will join later. We have called the place *High Fields*, in which there is a secret second meaning. It pleases me very much."

The Troopers followed suit at the end of the summer. In September 1933, the three troopers remaining at Highfields – William Sawyer, Joseph Wolf and John Genz – received their orders to return to their barracks. For thirty-one months the troopers lived in the "old yellow house that stands beside the bumpy road leading up to the big white farm house."

The Highfields Association, as the Trustees were called, was located in Weehawkin, New Jersey and Charles Lindbergh served as its president. In June 1940 Charles and Anne went to Breckinridge's law office in Manhattan "for a meeting on *High Fields,* to vote to turn over the place to New Jersey, who think they can use it for children. It is rather a gloomy meeting, full of ghosts – the ghost of people we used to be, relationships we used to have."

The house was turned over by the Association to the State of New Jersey for use "as a home for indigent children with heart ailments. Since the 1950s the home has been used as a juvenile rehabilitation center by the New Jersey Department of Corrections." Troubled juveniles are sent to Highfields by court order to complete a program of "mandated individualized education, community service, pre-vocational training and guided group interaction."

Difficult as it was to finally part with *High Fields*, Anne found that this was an opportunity to also part with the sadness that seemed to haunt the house. "Let the sorrow be wiped out, the horror wiped out, in a vital living good – a home for children."

Lindbergh's house still stands today, with some alterations. For example, the Southside of the house originally had a series of French doors leading to a walled patio. In the 1980s this area was enclosed to provide more living space. Below the servants' quarters in the east wing the three-car garage was also converted into living space.

A fire in 1984 destroyed what was once Lindbergh's library and damaged the window frames of the nursery above. The windows were replaced and the library was remodeled with wood paneling.

In August 1990, the house and program were dedicated to the memory of one of its directors, Albert D. Elias and is today known as *The Albert D. Elias Rehabilitation Group at Highfields.*

9. Al Reich

When the kidnapper(s) of the Lindbergh Baby accepted Doctor John F. Condon's offer to serve as their intermediary with the Lindberghs, they failed to consider one thing: Condon didn't own a car. Condon relied on family and friends to drive him to places the athletic septuagenarian could not reach on foot. One of his friends who served as chauffeur was former heavyweight boxer Al Reich. They had met sometime prior to 1925[15] and became the best of friends. In 1932, Al Reich lived at 415 Minnieford Avenue on City Island with his wife Agnes and mother. He drove a Ford coupe with a rumble seat and was constantly at Doctor Condon's side, especially during the Lindbergh Case. They were together so often that many people – including Jersey City Police Inspector Harry Walsh – believed that he was actually Condon's bodyguard.

Alfred Jacob Reich – the *blond Adonis* as he was known in the ring – was born in New York on March 11, 1890. Al Reich was "a power hitter with a hard punch in each hand; but he was temperamental and did not always follow the fight plan or fight with confidence." Nevertheless, Reich was the amateur heavyweight champion, having won the Amateur Championship of New York in 1912 and 1913 and both the Metropolitan Amateur Championship and the National Amateur Championship in Boston in 1913. Later that year, managed by Max Blumenthal, Reich went professional, fighting his first pro bout against Charles "Sailor" White on September 12th in New York City.

In a November 23, 1914 article, the New York Times wrote that Al Reich was the "most promising of aspiring white hope [boxers]" of the day. The "White Hope" era began in December 1908 when Jack Johnson, an African American, defeated Tommy Burns for the heavyweight championship. This was the first time a black man had won the championship and the "cry" that "went up for a 'white hope' to reclaim the title" was a sad reflection of the racism that was rampant not only in boxing but in society as a whole. It was not until April 5, 1915 when Jess Willard defeated Johnson that the "White Hope" era finally came to an end. The victory did not put an end to racist segregation in boxing, however, as evidenced by the fact that "from 1915 through 1935 very few black fighters got the chance to fight for a world crown."

Regardless of the era in which history placed his career, Al Reich was an honest pugilist. In February 1915, the New York State Athletic Commission dismissed charges that Reich "…had faked" and was pulling his punches in his fight with "Fireman" Jim Flynn on January 12th. According to the New York Times, "evidence was produced to show that Reich had injured his right hand in the encounter with Flynn, and after the third round was unable to use it effectively, thereby giving rise to the reports that he 'was pulling.'"

A one-time sparring partner for the great Jack Dempsey, Al Reich fought his last professional bout on April 5, 1924 against Luis Angel Firpo, the South American heavyweight champion, in Argentina. *The Wild Bull* knocked Reich out in the first round.

After hanging up his gloves, Al Reich continued to keep busy as a licensed referee for professional wrestling and boxing matches in New York State. Doctor Condon also got him interested in real estate and listed him as an associate in Condon's real estate business on City Island.

Al Reich was a minor character in the Lindbergh Case who, as stated before, was in the constant company of one of its major characters. He was at Doctor Condon's house "every day since the day after [Condon] received the first message from the kidnappers, going home around two or three o'clock every morning." On March 11th, it was to Al Reich that Doctor Condon turned when he needed a ride to Woodlawn Cemetery to meet with the kidnappers.

> Doctor Condon got in touch with me and asked me if I would drive him to a refreshment stand about 100 feet north of the last station on the Jerome Avenue subway…I drove him up there and I parked the car in front of this refreshment stand and he walked in on the porch and found [a] note under [a] rock where they had said it would be.

Other than Condon, Al Reich is the only person to have seen the mysterious *Cemetery John* – the alleged kidnap gang representative with whom Condon met and to whom he eventually turned over the ransom money.

Pretty soon a man appeared inside the cemetery at the gate waving a handkerchief to attract the Doctor's attention and the Doctor went over and spoke to him through the gate...After a little while the fellow climbed up and over the gate and, landing on the Doctor's side of the gate...started running...the doctor followed...caught up to him...and got him to sit down on a bench...where they conversed for about an hour. During this time I was sitting in my car about 100 yards away.

Reich was a Prosecution Witness at the trial of Bruno Richard Hauptmann, testifying on January 8th and 9th, 1935. He testified about driving Doctor Condon to the Woodlawn Cemetery meeting and also about the packages of ransom money that were assembled. He stated that they contained a total of $70,000. Asked by the Attorney General how it was he knew this he replied, "I was there when it was packed up!"

I drove down with Colonel Breckenridge to the banker's home and met with Colonel Lindbergh down there...we took the $50 (thousand) in Colonel Lindbergh's car and Colonel Breckenridge took the twenty in his.

Al Reich and his wife eventually moved away from City Island and they settled in the small village of Ossining, Westchester County, New York. The *Blond Adonis* heavyweight boxer passed away at his home on July 27, 1963. He was 73 years old. His wife survived him by 13 years. She died in September 1976 at the age of 77.

10. Betty Gow

Many of the servants employed by the Lindberghs and Morrows were immigrants from Europe, several from Great Britain. Betty Gow was the "Little Lindy's" nanny. She was born at 26 Polmadie Street in Glasgow, Scotland on February 12, 1904. Her mother was Isabella McLaglan. Her father, William Gordon Gow, was a baker. After he died, Betty's mother married John Tayler, a cabinetmaker. Betty was a member of the Govanhill Parish Church and she attended Wolseley Street and Haysfield Street public schools to the age of fourteen.

Betty worked as a sales girl in various stores in Glasgow. Her first job was as a dressmaker with Copland & Lyre, warehousemen, at 165 Sauchiehall Street. Six months later, she was working with the Kinning Park Co-Operative Society on Rutherglen Road as a cash girl. She left this job due to illness. Later, in 1923, she was employed by A. L. Scott, Boot Factors, on Argyle Street, first in the warehouse and later in their branch shop in Sauchiehall Street. She worked there for six years, quitting to move to America.

Betty immigrated to the United States on April 27, 1929 on the steamship Cameronia of the Anchor Line. She first came to Bogota, New Jersey where her brother, William, lived. Two days later she moved to Teaneck, New Jersey where she worked as a nanny for the Gibbs family. She then moved to Detroit where she was employed by the Adam Jackson family of Lakeweed Street. Mrs. Jackson was the sister-in-law of Betty's brother William.

After leaving the employment of the Jackson family, she worked for a few days with the Ross Family and later for the Moser Family of Grosse Pointe before returning to New Jersey in October 1930.

Once back in New Jersey, she obtained work through the Lydia Lonquist Employment Agency with Mrs. Warren Sullivan of Englewood. She worked there for nine months before taking the position of nanny with the Lindbergh family in 1931.

Betty was the last person to see the baby alive. She had put him to bed around 7:30 pm and when she returned to check on him at 10:00, she discovered he was missing. Naturally, the police wanted to thoroughly investigate her. During her interrogations, they learned that she was dating a Norwegian sailor who jumped ship in March 1927. An illegal alien, Finn Henrik (Henry) Johnson managed to secure a job on Thomas Lamont's yacht. In 1930, Betty was with the Lindbergh's at their summer retreat in North Haven, Maine. It was while here that she met "Red" Johnson who was also in North Haven with the Lamont's yacht.

Henry and Betty became prime suspects. Henry was arrested in Connecticut and interrogated and later released and he returned to Norway. Betty, too, was cleared of any compliance in the kidnapping by the New Jersey State Police. She continued in the employ of the Lindbergh's, caring for their second child, Jon, who was born in August 1932. She eventually moved back to Scotland, returning in 1935 to testify at the Hauptmann Trial.

After the trial of Richard Hauptmann, Betty Gow returned to Scotland and lived on Kings Park Avenue in Rutherglen, just outside Glasgow. She retired as a manager from the Ilene Adairs Dress Shop. She never married. Betty died on July 16, 1996 at the Victoria Infirmary Annex in Glasgow at the age of 92.

11. Olly and Elsie Whateley

Often in murder mysteries there is an obligatory (and somewhat cliché) butler, and the Lindbergh Case is no exception. In keeping with the cliché, the butler in the Lindbergh household was also English. In this case, however, the butler didn't "do it."

Olly Whateley was born in Handsworth, Birmingham, England, on June 18, 1884, the son of Henry Whateley and Emily Groves. He attended school up to the age of 15 when he transferred to a trade school, studying to become a jeweler. He served his apprenticeship with Tandy & Sons of Birmingham, and worked with them for about 20 years.

During the First World War,[16] Whateley was employed in the munitions plant in Birmingham. After the war, he started his own jewelry and ring maker business in Birmingham on Byse Street called "*Whateley and Smith.*" To this day, Vyse Street is in what is known as the "Jewelry Quarter" in the Hockley area of Birmingham. "After a slump in the trade, he opened up an outfitters shop on Hamstead Road, but did not do so well in the business."

In 1916, Olly married Elsie Marie Lee. A native of the Ladywood section of Birmingham, she was born on November 2, 1884. Like her future husband, she attended school to the age of 15 when she went into an office to work as a secretary. She then did clerical work for six years and also took singing lessons for eight years.

In 1926, Olly went to work for his wife's brother-in-law, George Albert Ward, who was the manager of Ward & Co Machine Shop on Dale Road in the Hornbrook section of Birmingham and was employed there until late 1929.

Leaving her brother William Glover Lee and sister Emily A. Lee Ward behind in Birmingham (both of their parents had died by this time), Elsie and her husband left England for a new life in the United States. After selling their home at No. 233 Balden Road in Harborne, Birmingham, to a Mr. Clements they set sail on the Cunard White Star Liner S. S. *Scythia* on March 1st. They sailed with two other couples, Charles and Ada Dyson and a "Mr. And Mrs. Tyler", both of Birmingham. The Atlantic crossing took about two weeks and they arrived in New York on March 12, 1930.

The Whateleys made their way to the home of Miss Valinsitz at 71 Franklin Avenue in New Rochelle, New York, with whom they stayed while registering with the Hutchinson Employment Agency on Madison Avenue in New York.

The agency found them both work in Mendham, New Jersey, where they were employed as the butler and housekeeper for Mr. J. H. Potter. They held these positions for about four months, when they voluntarily resigned and returned to the home of Miss Valinsitz in New Rochelle.

Two weeks later, Olly and Elsie took on a temporary job as caretakers of the Grosvenor estate in Old Westbury, Long Island. This job lasted four about seven weeks, through the dog days of August and September 1930.

Unemployed once again, they returned to New Rochelle. While waiting for word from the employment agency, Elsie took a job in the art department of Ware Stores Company in New Rochelle. In early October, just two weeks into this new job, the Whateleys received word from the Hutchinson Employment Agency that two caretaker positions were available at the Lindbergh home in Princeton, New Jersey. They were definitely interested in the job and on October 15, 1930 Colonel Lindbergh hired them surprisingly without a thorough background check.

When asked by Richard Hauptmann's attorney at the trial in Flemington about the hiring of the Whateleys, Colonel Lindbergh stated that he could not recall the name of the agency that had recommended them to him. "I don't recall the name of the agency," he said. "I recall talking to Mr. And Mrs. Whateley at the time, in my office." The Defense Attorney pressed his point: "What I am getting at, Colonel, is this: What investigation did you make of Whateley before you hired him as your butler…?" The Colonel replied simply, "I talked to him. Beyond that I never go any further. I think that [his background] may have been looked into. Personally I simply talked to Mr. And Mrs. Whateley for half an hour or an hour."

When the Whateleys were hired, the Lindbergh estate in Hopewell was still under construction, so they began their employment at *White Cloud Farm*, the house in nearby Lawrenceville that the Lindberghs were renting at the time. "I was the housekeeper and my husband drove the car and waited on the table and did anything that was needed around the house."

The Lindberghs would visit the house in Lawrenceville, and later the Hopewell house, on weekends. Usually Mrs. Lindbergh and the baby would stay over until Monday afternoon when Olly would drive her back to Englewood, returning home about six o'clock in the evening.

When Colonel Lindbergh hired the Whateleys, he agreed to their demand that they both be granted the same day off. It was either that "or we wouldn't take the position." This, however, led to a problem once they moved into the Hopewell House. Who would watch over the house when the Whateleys were off?

On four different occasions when the Whateleys were away from the Hopewell House, Ambrose J. Titus and his wife would be left in charge. Mr. and Mrs. Titus were both in their early seventies and lived about three miles away from the Lindberghs at 36 Columbia Avenue in downtown Hopewell. They lived in Hopewell and the surrounding area for the past sixty years and had a very good reputation in their community.

During the summer of 1932, the Whateleys were given six weeks vacation and they used this opportunity to return to England to visit family and friends. While they were away, the Hopewell House was watched over by George Springer and his family. When they returned, they continued in Lindbergh's employ as caretakers of the estate.

On March 10, 1933 Elsie once again sailed for England to visit family for several weeks in Birmingham. This time, however, Olly remained behind. One spring morning, Olly was at the Hopewell House when he started feeling sharp pains in his abdomen. He was rushed Princeton Hospital and on May 19th he underwent an operation for a perforated duodenal ulcer "…which Dr. Ralph Belford said had caused an 'acute condition in the abdomen.'" He remained in serious condition and, although he appeared to be improving, took a turn for the worse. At 11:20 in the morning of May 23rd, he passed away – the same day his wife arrived home. He was cremated the next day at the crematorium in Linden, New Jersey, under the direction of funeral director Samuel S. Mather of Princeton.

Elsie Whateley continued to work for the Lindbergh family and testified at the trial of Richard Hauptmann about the events at the Hopewell House surrounding the kidnapping of the Lindbergh Baby. Suffering from cancer, she returned to England after the trial and died on January 8, 1936.

12. Septimus Banks

On September 28, 1891 the great American novelist, Herman Melville, died in New York City. On that same day, several thousand miles away, in the east London borough of Hackney, Septimus Samuel Banks was born. The son of Samuel and Marian Laurence Banks, Septimus left school at the age of 15 to work for a Dr. Hanock in Leightonstone, London for three years. He then worked for two years for R. B. C. Chapman and later the Lady Donald Stewart, for about a year and eleven months.

For the next three years he worked for the Honourable Mrs. Morrison of 14 Grosvenor Crescent, London. After this, he spent four months working for Lord Islington[17] of Harman Park, Corsham who, at this time, was the Undersecretary of State for India.

After leaving Lord Islington's service Septimus moved to Scotland where he served Andrew Carnegie. On September 18, 1914, he immigrated to the United States on the R. M. S. Lusitania from Nornoch, Scotland. While in the United States, he continued to work for Andrew Carnegie for four and a half years at his residence at 2 East 91st Street in New York City.

During the First World War, he enlisted in the 70th Battery, Canadian Field Artillery as a gunner. When he returned from the war, he married Rose Flynn, a native of New York City and daughter of Irish immigrants in May 1918. Sadly, on the afternoon of November 21, 1929, Rose Banks died from *Delirium Tremens* caused by alcohol poisoning.[18] She was buried four days later in St. Raymond's Cemetery in the Bronx.

Banks was discharged from the Canadian Army on Christmas Day, 1918 and he returned to New York with his wife. In January 1919, he entered into service with Dwight Morrow. Dwight Morrow was a United States Senator living in Englewood, New Jersey. Septimus worked continuously for

Mr. Morrow until October 1927 when Senator Morrow was appointed as Ambassador to Mexico. Banks stayed behind and became a "free lance" in the catering business, working for Charles Welsh of 157 East 80th Street until June 1931 when he re-entered the service of the Morrow Family.

Upon their return from Mexico, Septimus served as both a butler and personal valet to Senator Morrow. Just a few months later, on October 4, 1931, he became the last person to see Dwight Morrow alive:

> Shortly before midnight on Sunday, October 4, 1931, Dwight Morrow leaned on the arm of his waiting valet and walked slowly up the stairs of his darkened house. Morrow usually wasn't one to lean, but he had never felt so tired. He and Banks climbed up the winding lantern-lit stairway to the second floor and turned toward the double wooden doors of the master suite. As Morrow wished banks a 'good night', Banks noted that Morrow looked uncommonly pale...

Around eleven the next morning, Morrow's secretary, Arthur Springer, and Septimus Banks entered the bedroom and found the Senator unconscious, the victim of a stroke. Two and a half hours later, Dwight Morrow died at Englewood Hospital.

Five months later, at approximately 10:00 A. M. on March 1, 1932 Septimus answered the telephone at the Morrow Estate in Englewood. On the phone was Anne Lindbergh, the daughter of Dwight and Elizabeth Morrow. She was calling from her new home in Hopewell, New Jersey. She requested to speak to Betty Gow, the nanny for her 20-month-old son, Charles A. Lindbergh, Jr. She was requesting that Betty be sent to Hopewell to help care for the baby since both the baby and Anne were suffering from a bad cold. It was later that night that the baby was kidnapped from his nursery.

Although Septimus was cleared as a suspect by the authorities, he was interrogated and his background was investigated. It was speculated that Septimus Banks was an alcoholic. In a 1932 FBI report, it was stated that Septimus was "employed off and on for a period of about fifteen years; had been discharged several times because of drunkenness and re-employed. At the time of the kidnapping, [he] had been steadily employed for four or five years. [He] is said to have done most of his drinking in a speakeasy in the Yorkville section of New York City around 70th Street...and that he was very talkative and quite irresponsible when drunk and on several occasions had to be loaded in a taxicab to be taken home."

Banks was also alleged to have frequented a Fort Lee, New Jersey speakeasy called the Sha-Toe, "a hang-out for horseplayers" and reportedly told the police he was there on the night of March 1, 1932.

According to one of his co-workers, Mrs. Marguerite Junge, "…none of the servants brought liquor to the estate with the exception of Banks, who besides drinking at speakeasies, occasionally had a bootlegger deliver liquor to him in bottles at the estate at night, and that the bootlegger would leave the bottles in a window where Banks could get it later…"

Marguerite Junge also told the FBI that after Dwight Morrow died in October 1931, "…one of the [Morrow] servants told [her] that…Septimus Banks, the butler, [was] left out of the will, but that it was believed that Senator Morrow had intended to make some provision for [him]. It was Mrs. Junge's opinion that Mrs. Morrow felt that if Banks received a large sum of money he would spend it in dissipation and that she kept him on as butler in spite of his drinking habits because of Senator Morrow's regard for him, and so that he would always have a home."

Septimus was also rumored to be the fiancé of Violet Sharp, a maid in the employ of the Morrow household. Miss Sharp was a prime suspect, for a while, in the Lindbergh Kidnapping Case because when was interrogated by the New Jersey State Police and Jersey City Police, she continuously lied, contradicted herself and misled the investigators. Finally, when the police called to schedule a fourth interview with her on 10 June 1932, she committed suicide by drinking potassium chloride – silver polish.

It was never ascertained for certain whether or not they were actually engaged however they were close friends. In an undated letter to Violet, her mother wrote: "I am glad to hear you are having a[n] easy time & Mr. Banks [is] looking after you that is jolly good." In Violet's May 24, 1932 interrogation she touched on their relationship by telling the police "we are just on friendly terms…ever since he has been [employed] there." Several times, she and Banks would "…walk outside around the Morrow estate… [and they] used to sit on the railing on the bridge."

According to the FBI Summary Report of February 1934, Septimus was "…reported to have entered a sanitarium, Central Park West, near 66th Street, and to have remained there two weeks during August 1932. Rumor prevalent among the Morrow servants is to the effect that the death of Violet Sharpe [sic] completely unnerved him. He is reported to have again spent some time in this sanitarium just prior to Christmas, 1932, as a result of overindulgence in alcoholic stimulants."

Septimus eventually left the Morrow household and moved to College Point, New York. On April 21, 1939 his former employer, Charles Welch in New York City, once again employed him. In 1942, at the age of 50, Septimus registered for the Selective Service. After the United States entered World War II in December 1941, all men between the ages of 45 and 64 were required to register for the Draft. Known as "The Fourth Registration" (or colloquially, as "The Old Man's Registration"), this registration was conducted on April 27, 1942. At this time, Septimus was living at 304 East 72nd Street in New York and he worked at 141 East 56th Street.

Unfortunately, nothing else is known of Septimus Banks except that he died in Matawan, New Jersey in January 1970 at the age of 79.

1. Henry "Red" Johnson (sitting) on Thomas Lamont's yacht *Reynard*

2. "Red" Johnson shortly before his death

3. Hauptmann's Car

4. Left to Right: Attorney General David T. Wilentz, Anthony Hauck, Jr., and Robert Peacock

5. John F. "Jafsie" Condon
In the bottom photo he is "demonstrating" how Cemetery John wore
his hat and pulled up his coat collar to conceal his face.

6. Highfields

**7. Al Reich – former boxer and, according to his 1914
draft registration card, a medical school student!**

8. Betty Gow   **9. Septimus S. Banks**

10. Olly Whateley (holding Wahgoosh) and Elsie Whateley

11. Olly Whateley at
Highfields

12. Trooper Wolf with Elsie
Whateley at Highfields

13. Henry Breckinridge

Colonel Henry Breckinridge was Charles Lindbergh's personal attorney and confidant. In fact, just after Olly Whateley the butler called the Hopewell Police, Breckinridge was the first person Lindbergh phoned on the night of the kidnapping. The two had met shortly after Lindbergh's flight in 1927. A year earlier, Daniel Guggenheim established a "Fund for the Promotion of Aeronautics." After Lindbergh returned from Paris, the Fund asked him to "embark on a three-month tour that would take the *Spirit of St. Louis* to all forth-eight states in the Union." When Lindbergh agreed to the tour he hired Breckinridge, who was Guggenheim's attorney, "...to act as his personal advisor, to sort through the hundreds of offers coming his way and to challenge the hundreds of illegal abuses of Lindbergh's name in promoting products."

Five years later, Breckinridge served as Lindbergh's closest advisor during the investigation of the kidnapping. Anne Lindbergh wrote to her mother-in-law that, "Col. Henry has hardly slept for six days. I am worried about him and C[harles] counts on his judgment." It was that closeness that almost got Colonel Breckinridge and his wife Aida into trouble with Colonel H. Norman Schwarzkopf of the State Police and the Attorney General. The Breckinridges were the only non-family members with exclusive access to the Lindberghs and it was they – and not the police – who were advising them on what they should do.

For example, it was Breckinridge that small time mobster Morris "Mickey" Rosner contacted and told that he would be able to help solve the case by way of his contacts in the underworld. Breckinridge convinced Lindbergh to accept his offer and also convinced Lindbergh to provide Rosner with a $2,500 expense account.

Later, after Rosner fell by the wayside, Breckinridge worked closely with the newly appointed intermediary, Dr. John F. Condon. "Colonel Henry" found himself in the thick of the ransom negotiations, spending what seemed to be more time at Dr. Condon's home than his own!

By the middle of March, 1932 Schwarzkopf felt that the Breckinridges' closeness and advice were interfering too much with the investigation. On March 22nd, he met with the Attorney General to discuss what should be done:

> I...asked him what action to take with regard to Colonel Breckinridge [and] Mrs. Breckinridge...and anyone else who had been in conference with the members of the household...I [also] inquired as to who should be held on charges of conspiracy, compounding a felony or anything else of this kind in case the payment of the ransom was negotiated and the child returned.

Unfortunately the Attorney General's recommendations are not recorded, but this demonstrates the frustration felt by the State Police superintendent at his exclusion from the conferences held between Lindbergh and his inner circle. While not actually confirmed, it is likely that Lindbergh himself would have stepped in to smooth things over with Schwarzkopf, and once the ransom was paid and the child's remains discovered in the woods, Lindbergh and his inner circle had little influence on the investigation.

Like Doctor Condon, Breckinridge's role is extensively discussed in almost every book written about the Lindbergh Case. However, not much is written about whom this prominent Manhattan attorney actually was.

Henry Breckinridge was a Presbyterian of Scots-Irish descent. His earliest American ancestor emigrated from Northern Ireland to Pennsylvania in 1728. The family later moved to Virginia and then Kentucky. But it was in Chicago, Illinois that on May 25, 1886 Henry was born to Major General Joseph Cabell and Louise Dudley Breckinridge, one of thirteen children, nine of whom survived past infancy.

By the time of Henry's birth, the Breckinridges had become a political dynasty, a family steeped in the tradition of public and military service. This fact was not lost on Henry. In 1907 he graduated from Princeton University and then attended Harvard Law School where he received his LL.B in 1910. He was admitted to the Kentucky Bar and had his practice in Lexington for three years.

Then, in 1913, when he was just 27 years old, President Woodrow Wilson appointed him Assistant Secretary of War. The following year, as World War

I broke out in Europe, Breckinridge was sent to Europe with a group of military officers and consular representatives. Sailing on two destroyers, their mission was to deliver over $3 million in gold to American refugees – mostly tourists – that were trying to flee the war zone.

By the end of 1915 both Breckinridge and his boss, Secretary of War Lindley Garrison, were at odds with the President over the state of the military. Wilson had a policy of strict neutrality and promised to keep the United States out of the war in Europe. Garrison and Breckinridge strongly believed "that a full-time reserve army should be created as a foundation for national defense and…for support in case the United States entered the European war." Finally, on February 10, 1916 Secretary Garrison resigned followed shortly thereafter by Henry Breckinridge.

The President accepted both resignations immediately. He wrote to Breckinridge that "I do so with genuine regret, because you have in every way fulfilled the highest expectations and rendered the country the most conscientious and efficient service. It is with genuine sorrow that I see this official relationship between us brought to an end."

Henry spent the rest of the year serving as the vice president of the Pacific Hardware & Steel Company in San Francisco, California. When the United States entered the war in 1917, he joined an officers' training camp and was commissioned as a major in the infantry, and by the end of the war, he had been promoted to the rank of Lieutenant Colonel. He was sent overseas with the American Expeditionary Force in command of a battalion and saw action in the *Vosges*, at *St. Mihiel* and in the *Meuse-Argonne* Offensive.

After the war, Henry was honorably discharged in 1919. He returned to civilian life and practiced law in Washington, D. C., until 1922 when he moved to New York City. He continued his practice in Manhattan until his death. While living in Washington, Breckinridge also served as president of the Navy League (1919-1921) and organized the first Navy Day celebration.

During the 1920s, Henry Breckinridge not only made a name for himself in the legal profession but also in the world of sports. In 1920 the former Assistant Secretary of War was selected to represent his country as a member of the US Olympic Fencing Team at the VII Olympiad at Antwerp, Belgium.

> Competing in the preliminary round of the annual national foils fencing championship tournament at the New York A[thletic] C[lub], the former War Department official, wearing the emblem of the Army Officers' Fencing Club of Washington, DC, went through the first round with flying

colors…His record for the day showed Breckinridge had won nine bouts and lost two.

This should come as no surprise. Henry's brother, Dr. Scott D. Breckinridge, was an Olympic fencer and, in 1941, co-authored with his son the book *Sword Play*. He was also the coach of the University of Kentucky Fencing Team.

Henry himself had been involved with fencing for many years and in January 1914 he served as Secretary of the recently reorganized Fencers' Club in Washington, DC. In addition to 1920, he was a member of the US Olympic Fencing Team in 1924 and served as the team captain in 1928. In 1920 he was also a member of the Olympic bronze medal winning foil team.

From 1925 to 1930, Henry served as president of the American Fencing League Association (AFLA) and was the AFLA national outdoor epee champion in 1930. He was also a six-time national medalist in foil and epee.

Henry Breckinridge re-entered the political arena in the 1930s. In 1932 he managed Harry F. Byrd's unsuccessful campaign for the presidential nomination at the Democratic Convention. Two years later, he himself ran for Senate as an Independent in an attempt to "resist the Tammanyzing of the United States"; however, his newly formed *Constitutional Party* was defeated at the polls.

In 1936 Breckinridge ran for president, entering the Democratic Presidential Primaries in Maryland, New Jersey, Ohio and Pennsylvania on an anti-New Deal platform. Mark Sullivan of the *Charleston Daily Mail* wrote,

> No one has the faintest expectation that Colonel Breckinridge will win the primary or come anywhere near winning it. If, however, in this comparatively small state [of Maryland] he should get as many as 15 or 20 thousand votes, or as much as 10% of the total Democratic votes cast, such an outcome would cause serious concern to Mr. Roosevelt…The votes that Colonel Breckinridge gets in Maryland will be purely anti-Roosevelt votes…In offering himself as a candidate for the Democratic Presidential nomination…he does so wholly for the purpose of giving to Democrats who disapprove the New Deal a chance to register a protest vote.

Once again, Breckinridge did not win but he did receive 16% of the vote in Maryland.

According to biographer Scott Berg, Breckinridge's friendship with Lindbergh began to fade, "especially after the lawyer entered politics." By the late 1930s, Lindbergh became an outspoken proponent of isolationism, serving as spokesman of the America First movement. In an interesting parallel to his opposition of President Wilson in the run-up to the First World War, this attitude led Breckinridge to resign as Lindbergh's attorney and to oppose him publicly, going as far as to say,

> Norway has its Quisling. France its Laval. The United States has its equivalent. He who spreads the gospel of defeatism is an ally of Adolf Hitler. All those who are not with Hitler are against him.

In January 1939, Breckinridge sent Lindbergh, who was now living in France, a long letter chiding him for his politics. Anne wrote that the hurtful letter "…is the most depressing thing in the mail. He opposes C[harles] at every point."

The following year, Anne wrote in her diary that it was "announced on the radio…from Washington that two friends close to Colonel Lindbergh would speak against his point of view this week – Colonel Henry and Mother!"

It was around this time, in 1940, that Breckinridge separated from his second wife. He ended up marrying a total of three times. He married his first wife, Ruth Bradley Woodman, a Concord, New Hampshire native, on July 7, 1910 in Geneva, Switzerland. They had two children, Louise Dudley Breckinridge and Elizabeth Foster Breckinridge.

Henry and Ruth divorced in 1925. On July 20, 1934 their eldest daughter, Louise, was killed in a tragic shooting accident. Louise was living with her mother in Bethesda, Maryland at the time and enjoyed taking evening walks to go target shooting. On this particular evening she left around 6:00 PM with her two dogs and a .22-calibre target rifle. According to a *New York Times* article, "she had walked several blocks, and had reached a wooded area. As she climbed a fence, her rifle apparently became entangled and she fell, discharging the weapon. The bullet entered her left breast and reached her heart. She is believed to have died instantly."

About an hour and forty-five minutes after she left home, her mother went looking for her, concerned that she had not returned. She found her daughter lying about five feet from the fence. She called for help, but her daughter was already dead.

Several years later, tragedy struck the family again. In 1941 Ruth was reported missing from a ship that authorities believed was sunk by a German U-Boat, just prior to the United States entering the Second World War.

Henry's second wife was socialite Aida de Acosta. Born in Elberton, New Jersey on July 28, 1884 she was the daughter of a Cuban-born father. She attended school at the Sacred Heart Convent in Paris where she became friends with Alberto Santos-Dumont. He was a Brazilian aviator and, after receiving training from him, Aida became the first woman aviator to pilot a motorized airship. On July 9, 1903 she flew one of his dirigibles five miles from Paris to Bagatelle, landing in a polo field where she interrupted an important match between the United States and England.

Aida Breckinridge spent most of her life leading various charities and social organizations, but her most important work was as the executive director of the Eye Bank for Sight Restoration, an organization she helped establish after she had her glaucoma cured by Dr. William Wilmer of Washington. "Through former patients and friends, she led a campaign that raised $3,000,000 to establish the Wilmer Ophthalmological Institute at Johns Hopkins University, as a teaching and research center, and the first eye institute in the country."

Aida had been married to Oren Root, the president of the Hudson and Manhattan Rail Road. After their mutual divorces, Aida and Henry Breckinridge were married on August 5, 1927. They separated on July 2, 1940,[19] but it was not until March 25, 1947 that their divorce was finalized in Reno, Nevada. Two days after his divorce, Henry married his third wife, Margaret Lucy Smith in Carson City, Nevada. They had one daughter, Madeline.

Henry Breckinridge continued to work in his law offices at 24 West 40th Street in Manhattan while he and Margaret took up residence in Fresh Meadows, Queens at 67-38B 190th Lane. On May 2, 1960 he drove himself from his home to St. Vincent's Hospital for a routine check-up. While there he suddenly became ill and died. Henry Breckinridge was 73 years old.

14. The "Triumvirate of Intermediaries"

It is often forgotten that there were in fact two trials held in the Flemington Court House in connection with the Lindbergh Case. The most famous, of course, was the 1935 "Trial of the Century" of Bruno Richard Hauptmann. But there was an earlier trial, one that became known as "The Hoax Trial." During the summer of 1932 John Hughes Curtis, a ship builder from Norfolk, Virginia, was placed on trial for obstructing justice while perpetrating a hoax against Colonel Lindbergh.

In March 1932 John Hughes Curtis contacted Charles Lindbergh and informed him that the actual kidnappers of Lindbergh's son had contacted him. According to Curtis' story, late in the evening of March 9th, a local bootlegger he knew approached him in the parking lot of a local marina. He said that he was acting as a go-between for the kidnappers of Colonel Lindbergh's baby and that they wanted to get in touch with Lindbergh to discuss the ransom payment and return of the baby. They wanted John H. Curtis to contact Lindbergh on their behalf. Curtis told the man that he wanted absolutely nothing to do with this.

Curtis lay awake all night thinking about the matter. "Early in the morning, I called Dean Dobson-Peacock and asked him to come over and see me…He came over…and I went into detail. We decided that the only thing to do was to try and get in touch with Lindbergh."

The two tried telephoning Colonel Lindbergh but Morris "Mickey" Rosner, the small time Mafioso whom Lindbergh temporarily appointed as his "private secretary", intercepted their call. "Our conversation was extremely unsatisfactory…[so] we decided to write a letter and address it to Mrs.

Morrow" whom the Dean knew. When this failed, Curtis' wife suggested that they contact Admiral Guy H. Burrage. "The Dean and I got in touch with Burrage and [he] agreed to get in touch with Lindbergh by phone. This was Saturday, March 19th. When this failed, Admiral Burrage wrote a letter to Lindbergh "...advising that we would arrive in Hopewell on Tuesday, March 22nd...we were stopped by a State Trooper at the entrance of the estate and Burrage gave his name. We were told to come to the house and report to the Trooper stationed in the garage. We were [then] ushered into the library... Colonel Lindbergh came in and very smilingly greeted Admiral Burrage." Success at last!

John Hughes Curtis proceeded to tell Lindbergh all he knew from the intermediary he had met. Lindbergh reluctantly agreed that Curtis might have been contacted by the kidnappers but told him that he needed further proof, a comment about the ransom money and photographs of the child. Curtis said he would see what he could do, and the Norfolk Triumvirate of Intermediaries, as one newspaper later called them, took their leave.

Shortly after returning to Virginia, Curtis told Dean Dobson-Peacock his contact that knew the kidnappers told him that the gang would accept $25,000. The Dean agreed to take the message to Lindbergh personally. He flew from the US Naval Air Station in Norfolk through a dangerous storm to the Philadelphia Naval Yard where an official US Navy car drove him to Highfields. Lindbergh and the State Police were still very skeptical about Curtis. When Dean Dobson-Peacock arrived at Highfields, he had difficulty convincing the Troopers on duty to let him pass. "While the chauffeur was arguing with the trooper [at the gate] Mr. Dobson-Peacock got out and demanded that he be permitted to use the telephone in the gatehouse." After some further squabbling, he was reluctantly allowed to use the emergency field phone to place a call to Colonel Breckinridge who then instructed the Troopers to open the gate and allow the Dean to pass. He related the message to Lindbergh who thanked him, and left the room. The Dean then got back into the car and returned to Philadelphia where he spent the night at the Rittenhouse Square Hotel, returning to Norfolk late the following morning. "He had scarcely departed [from Highfields] before Colonel H. Norman Schwarzkopf, Superintendent of the State Police...issued a statement at Trenton, discounting once more the importance of the information [Dean] Dobson-Peacock had brought. The statement merely said: 'Colonel Lindbergh does not believe the information obtained at Norfolk to be of specific significance in this case.'"

Regardless, Curtis continued to weave his elaborate hoax. "'Let them scoff. They have done everything they could to block us.'" Over the next two months, continued to lead Dean Dobson-Peacock and Admiral Burrage into believing his tale and convincing Lindbergh into chasing phantoms and ghost ships from New York City to Cape May, New Jersey, to the open seas. He somehow convinced Lindbergh to make at least eight trips to sea looking for the kidnappers' boat. It was not until after William Allen found the remains of Lindbergh's son in the woods near Hopewell on May 12th that the hoax was exposed and Curtis broke down and confessed.

On May 17, 1932 John Hughes Curtis, after some intimidation, admitted to the State Police that he concocted the entire elaborate scheme on his own:

> At that time I was having a great deal of worry and troubles, which was due to me having a nervous breakdown about a year ago...We were talking in the office and [someone] stated that as I knew a number of the people who might be interested in [the crime], especially rum runners, they probably would not object talking to me about going as a contact between them...I think it started to pry on my mind and the more I thought about it the more I was convinced that it might...be able to happen and with that in mind I went to Dean Dobson-Peacock...I told him that I had been approached by this man [who was the go-between]...It was absolutely just the result of a distorted mind.

Curtis was arrested and placed in the Flemington jail where he was held on $10,000 bail which, according to attorney C. Lloyd Fisher, was "the largest sum, so far as I know, ever named in a misdemeanor case." His attorney, W. L. Pender of Norfolk, retained local Flemington defense attorney C. Lloyd Fisher on behalf of Curtis. Fisher would go on to assist in the defense of Bruno Richard Hauptmann at his trial in the same Flemington Court House three years later.

According to Fisher, the State created the impression that they were going to prosecute John Hughes Curtis as a "hoaxer." "They went before the grand jury and had Curtis indicted on the ground that he did *not* know the kidnapers as he claimed." However, at the last minute the prosecution changed their view and "...they came to court prepared to prove that Curtis was *not* a hoaxer, that he *did* know the kidnapers, and that he was obstructing justice by refusing to disclose their whereabouts." Fisher had no defense against this accusation since it was exactly what he was preparing to prove. "All the defense could do, under the circumstances, was to put on a character witness or two, and rest."

On July 1, 1932 John Hughes Curtis was found guilty of obstruction of justice and sentenced to serve one year in prison. He was also fined $1,000. The prison term was suspended and as soon as he paid his fine, Curtis returned to Norfolk, Virginia.

How was it that a wealthy yet relatively unknown shipbuilder from Norfolk, Virginia, was able to gain the confidence of Colonel Charles Lindbergh? Finding a shipbuilder, a priest and an admiral on your doorstep one afternoon sounds more like the beginning of a joke or chapters in *The Canterbury Tales* than anything else. So who were these Magi that came knocking on Lindbergh's door?

John Hughes Curtis was 45 years old in 1932. Born in Portsmouth, Virignia, he lived most of his life in Norfolk. He was active in motorboat and yacht racing and was commodore of the local yacht club. He got into the shipbuilding and repair business in 1917 and was president of the Gas Engine and Boat Company "which constructed 300 outboard motor boats for Germany in 1928." This company, however, went bankrupt, a victim of the Great Depression. He then established the Curtis Boat Building Corporation "located on what is known as The Hauge, a small body of water which can be navigated only by vessels of light draft."

Curtis married Constance Robeteau of Brooklyn, New York, sometime around 1917. They had two children: a son, John H. Jr., who was born in 1920, and Constance, born in 1924.

Curtis was often away on business trips and "his business brought him in contact with all classes of persons who follow the water for their livelihood. He has repaired a number of coast guard craft and boats seized as rum runners." Business was not good and the family eventually had to move from the exclusive residential area in Algonquin Park to an apartment building at Redgate Avenue and Manteo Street.

Curtis' first attempt at reaching Lindbergh was through the Very Reverend Harold Dobson-Peacock. Born in 1880, Dobson-Peacock was an Anglican priest from England. He served with Canadian forces during the First World War and was wounded twice, having been shot in the shoulder and right arm.

He was called to be the Dean of the Episcopal Cathedral in Mexico City. It was during this time that he became acquainted with the Morrow Family as Charles Lindbergh's future father-in-law, Dwight Morrow, Sr., served as the American ambassador to Mexico.

In 1927, Dobson-Peacock was called to be the rector of the affluent Christ Church in Norfolk, Virginia.[20] The Dean, his wife and their daughter, Marjorie, lived in a rectory just a few yards from the church.

Dean Dobson-Peacock had rather liberal leanings, openly advocating for "Sunday morning moving pictures and baseball and declaring Prohibition to be the most 'asinine law ever imposed on a liberty-loving people.'"

After the First World War, he applied to join the American Legion, however his application was declined because he was not an American citizen and he did not serve with the American forces during the War.

On January 18, 1936 the ailing King George V approved the appointment of Dobson-Peacock to the vicarage St. Barnabas Church in Derbyshire, England.

It was Rear Admiral Burrage that had the closest relationship with Colonel Lindbergh. Born on June 14, 1967 in Lowell, Massachusetts, to Hamilton and Mary Howe Davis Burrage, Guy Hamilton Burrage graduated from the United States Naval Academy in 1887. He served as a midshipman aboard the frigate *Lancaster* on which he took his first transatlantic crossing. During the Spanish-American War, he served on the *Wheeling* in the North Pacific. From 1905-1907 he was the Executive Officer of the *Chattanooga* and in 1910 served as Executive Officer of the *Connecticut*. His first command was of the *Albatross* from 1910 to 1912. During the First World War, Burrage commanded the *Nebraska*.

After the end of the war, in 1919, he was stationed at the Norfolk Navy Yards as commandant. George Curtis, Sr. was chief clerk of the Norfolk Navy Yard at this time and it was through him that he met his son, John Hughes Curtis. Burrage was eventually transferred out and became the President of the Board of Inspection and Survey until he was relieved in 1926. At this time, he was promoted to Vice Admiral and he replaced Vice Admiral Roger Welles as Commandant of Naval Forces in Europe.

In June 1927, the cruiser Memphis was selected to bring aviator Charles Lindbergh home after his famous flight to Paris. As head of the Naval Forces in Europe, Admiral Burrage served as "Lucky Lindy's" escort. It was Vice Admiral Burrage that arranged the first meeting aboard the Memphis between Colonel Lindbergh and his mother upon his return to the States.

In September 1928, Admiral Burrage relinquished command of the European Fleet to Vice Admiral John H. Dayton. Sailing home on the former flagship *Detroit*, he assumed command of the Fifth Naval District with headquarters at Hampton Roads, Norfolk, Virginia. He held this post until his retirement on June 1, 1931, having served 44 years in the United States Navy.

Admiral Burrage retired in Norfolk and he incorporated the shipping crate for Lindbergh's plane, [the] *Spirit of St. Louis*, into a summer cottage in Contookcook, New Hampshire. It was here that he died on June 16, 1954.

By calling on the Dean and the Admiral, John Hughes Curtis was able to gain access to Lindbergh, however it has never really been explained why Lindbergh believed Curtis' story. What shibboleth did Curtis provide that convinced Lindbergh to even partially buy into his hoax?

Both Dean Dobson-Peacock and Admiral Burrage were cleared of any conspiracy and obstruction charges. It was evident that they, too, were the unwitting victims of Curtis' cruel hoax. Perhaps it was because they lived in a less cynical time and they truly believed it was their duty to come to Lindbergh's aid; that they were, in fact, acting out of a sense of humanity wanting to help the great American hero.

Ironically it was Dobson-Peacock who had encouraged Curtis on that March evening saying, "You have no choice. To refuse [to help] would be inhuman. It would cause you to regret the rest of your life." And regret they did.

15. Col. H. Norman Schwarzkopf

The son of German immigrants, jeweler Julius George Schwarzkopf and his wife Agnes lived in Newark, New Jersey. Their only son, Herbert Norman Schwarzkopf, was born on August 28, 1895. He was known, however, as "H. Norman" for two reasons. First, he wanted to emulate his father, who went by the name J. George Schwarzkopf, and secondly because he absolutely despised the name Herbert and all of the associated nicknames that went with it.

H. Norman Schwarzkopf attended local schools in Newark, including Barringer High School. After graduation, he was appointed to the West Point Military Academy on June 14, 1913. He excelled in sports, if not academics, and he developed a strong respect for the rules and regulations of the Academy, a respect that he would later instill on the Troopers of the New Jersey State Police.

Second Lieutenant Schwarzkopf graduated 88th in a class of 136. He was commissioned in the cavalry and served in the Second Cavalry at Fort Ethan Allen in Vermont. Eventually the Second Cavalry was converted to the 76th Field Artillery and they began training at camp Shelby, Mississippi.

With the First World War already raging for nearly four years in Europe, Schwarzkopf and his fellow comrades in arms were sent to the Western Front, arriving in France in May 1918 where they became part of the newly created Third Division. They first saw action two months later, during the *Second Battle of the Marne*. This was Germany's last major offensive on the Western Front and it lasted from July 15 through August 5, 1918. Most of the Allied casualties were inflicted upon the French, who suffered 95,000 casualties and losses. One of the American casualties was Captain Norman Schwarzkopf who was wounded in a gas attack. He recovered and was able to rejoin his regiment a short time later.

After the war, Schwarzkopf was stationed in Germany as part of the Army of Occupation, serving as Provost Marshal. He remained there for two years and in 1920 he was assigned to the 7th Cavalry at Fort Bliss, Texas, where he served as Assistant Provost Marshal for the El Paso District.

Shortly after his return to the United States Schwarzkopf learned that his father had been stricken by a "disabling illness." Feeling a strong sense of duty, Norman resigned from the army on April 15th and returned home to New Jersey to help care for his ailing father.

At the same time Schwarzkopf was caring for his father, the New Jersey Legislature was voting on what became known as the State Police Bill. This bill, when it was eventually passed into law over the Governor's veto, established a state police agency in New Jersey for the first time.

New Jersey Governor Edward I. Edwards needed to not only appoint a superintendent but also someone who could take the abstract ideas from the law and make the agency a reality. He picked 25-year-old H. Norman Schwarzkopf for that job. Reluctant at first, Schwarzkopf finally accepted and on July 1, 1921 he was sworn-in as the first Colonel and Superintendent of the New Jersey State Police.

Schwarzkopf now faced the daunting task of creating the State Police from the ground up, so it is not surprising that he based much of "the Outfit" on what he had learned at West Point and in the cavalry under General Pershing's leadership. He created a quasi-military organization steeped in the traditions of honor, duty and fidelity – the code that the New Jersey State Troopers live by still today.

While the history of the New Jersey State Police and its role in the Lindbergh Case is not within the scope of this book, it should be pointed out that the organization has evolved through trial and error over the years while it strives to meet the needs of the citizens of the State – and evolution that continues into the 21st Century.

The Lindbergh Kidnapping Case was not the first controversial case faced by the State Police but it was by far the largest and most important in the organizations eleven-year history. It also put a great strain on the organization. At least thirteen Troopers -- 5% of the entire State Police enlistment -- were assigned to the Lindbergh Case. To do that today would require over 380 Troopers to be assigned to the detail. That is more than the entire compliment of the Department of State Police in 1932.

One strange twist to the Lindbergh Case came to light in a New York Evening Journal article on February 16, 1935. Sid Boehm interviewed Schwarzkopf who had spent three years directing the investigation of the Lindbergh Kidnapping Case. Although there was an arrest, conviction and execution, Schwarzkopf had been accused by the governor and many in the public for "the most bungled police job in history." One of the biggest controversies of the case was the fact that Schwarzkopf allowed Colonel Charles Lindbergh to basically run the investigation. Schwarzkopf explained that "'I have gained a friend. There is nothing I wouldn't do for Colonel Lindbergh – there is no oath that I wouldn't break if it would materially help his well-being. There is not a single man in my outfit who wouldn't lay down his life for Colonel Lindbergh.'" He went on to say that "'I admit that there wasn't one single important step taken by us… until we consulted Colonel Lindbergh to learn if we would be interfering with his chances of getting back the baby. Of course, when the child was found, we knew we had waited vainly.'"

This outraged Governor Harold G. Hoffman. So much so that in June 1936 when Schwarzkopf's third term as superintendent expired, Hoffman refused to re-appoint him. Hoffman had been very vocal in his criticism of Schwarzkopf's handling of not only the Lindbergh Case but of other issues since the founding of the organization.

It should be noted that prior to Hoffman being elected governor, he was the head of the Motor Vehicle Bureau. As such, he had many run-ins with the Superintendent of the State Police. "There had been bad feelings between [Hoffman] and the police superintendent over limiting the role of Motor Vehicle Bureau personnel in police matters." Many felt that Hoffman's failure to re-appoint Schwarzkopf was the governor's way at seeking revenge against him. If true, Hoffman failed to heed the old saying that what you leave behind you, you will find in front of you.

When Schwarzkopf left State Police service that summer, he was hired by the Middlesex Transportation Company of New Brunswick and served as their vice president, later going on to become president of the company. He also lent his voice to narrate the famous radio show *Gang Busters* for a short time.

Eventually H. Norman Schwarzkopf re-entered the military and joined the New Jersey National Guard. He was promoted to Lieutenant Colonel and later Brigadier General. During the Second World War, General George Marshall sent Schwarzkopf to Iran as an advisor to the Imperial Iranian Gendarmerie.[21]

After the war, Schwarzkopf was once again stationed in Germany with the Army of Occupation. As Assistant Provost Marshall in the American Zone of Occupation, he was given the task of combating the black market. Later, he established a highway police force for the army, not surprisingly modeled after the New Jersey State Police.

When he returned to the Untied States in 1951, Schwarzkopf was appointed as the administrative director of the newly created Department of Law and Public Safety. As such, he coordinated investigations of frauds and waterfront crime in Hudson County and secured over sixty indictments.

One of his major investigations was into the charges of official misconduct by the recently suspended director of the Division of Employment Security. Files were seized and the financial records of the agency were audited. Schwarzkopf was hot on the trail of Division Director Harold G. Hoffman, the former governor, when on June 4, 1954 Hoffman was found dead in his room at the Blake Hotel in New York City. He had apparently died from a massive heart attack.

The investigation continued and eventually revealed "evidence of payroll padding, improper use of state employees and equipment, and payment for purchases that were never delivered." A confession in a letter to his daughter also revealed that the former governor had embezzled $300,000 from the South Amboy Bank where he was an officer in the 1920s.

In January 1956 Schwarzkopf retired from State service. He died unexpectedly two years later from a perforated ulcer at his home in West Orange, New Jersey. He left behind a legacy of leadership and devotion to duty that lives on in the 21st Century embodied in the proud traditions of the New Jersey State Police.

16. Hugo Stockburger[22]

Major Hugo Stockburger was just a young five-year veteran of the New Jersey State Police in 1934 when he received orders to guard Bruno Richard Hauptmann in the Flemington jail. That detail secured him a place in the history books. But Stockburger is one of those rare people whose life story reads like a history book in its own right.

There was no television. There wasn't even radio. Telephones were rare. Airplanes and automobiles were almost unheard of and Kaiser Wilhelm II was on the throne. It was into this world that Hugo Stockburger was born on December 28, 1906 in *Heutingsheim*, a small village in the state of *Württemberg* in southern Germany to Karl and Emilie Stockburger.

When the world went to war in 1914, Stockburger was just eight years old. The soldiers leaving to fight in the "war to end all wars" were sent off with brass bands and cheers. The martial spirit ran strong in Europe.

Stockburger remembers when the soldiers would come through his village on horseback. "The soldiers would ride through the village and they would pick up the kids along the way and let us ride on the horses with them until they reached the edge of town." Like children today, who put their ears to railroad tracks to listen for on-coming trains, Stockburger would put his ear to the tracks, too. But instead of he rumble of steam engines, he would hear the percussions of the massive rail guns being fired at the Western Front.

Unfortunately, there were more ominous and tragic memories of this, the first of the World Wars. Although his father went off to fight in the war, the government did not provide the soldiers' wives with any money, so Stockburger's mother had to go to work to support him and his sister, Hedwig. "We had ration cards. Many a night I remember my mother out in the kitchen making herself busy while my sister and I were eating. I would holler, 'Mom, aren't you hungry?' and she would always say, 'No, I'm not hungry.' But the truth was that there wasn't enough food."

During the last two months of the war, his sister Hedwig went out to watch the planes that were flying overhead on their way to bombing the village and a stray bomb killed her. "My parents carried her back into the house and she died in the basement. She was the only sister I had. And she had a baby boy. My parents raised him and my nephew is the only family I have left over there. I remember war. I want no part of it."

The war ended on November 11, 1918 with the signing of the Armistice in a railroad car in Versailles, France at 11:00 in the morning. Germany was devastated by its loss. Its economy was in shambles. Unemployment and inflation were rampant. The brass bands and cheers were silent. It was because of these conditions that Stockburger found himself aboard the *SS Sierra Ventana* sailing from Bremen for the United States. He arrived at Ellis Island on November 26, 1923 with just $25 in his pocket.

Hugo Stockburger's aunt, Friederike Lang, had paid for his passage and it was with her that he lived at 21 Sheridan Avenue in Trenton, New Jersey. While living with his aunt, he worked at the Scammell Pottery on 3rd Street in Trenton as a kiln man. Beginning in 1924 one of his jobs was to carry pottery around on his head in heavy clay boxes. "It really pressed into your scalp. That's how I started losing my hair."

Work at the pottery was not steady, though. Often, there were periods when the workers were laid off, then recalled only to be laid-off once again. In 1927 he saw an advertisement in the Trenton Times. The State Police needed a cook in their mess hall.

Stockburger worked in the kitchen at the State Police Training School Mess Hall in what would become West Trenton. Mrs. Grace Mulvey was the head cook at the time and when she took a day off, Stockburger would do the cooking. To get to work, he would take the bus from the intersection of State and Broad Streets in downtown Trenton to the Training School. A couple of times he missed it and he would walk the six miles to work. "I was in good shape!" he proclaimed later in his life.

At this time, the Department Headquarters building of the State Police was located on West State Street, across from the State House. Colonel H. Norman Schwarzkopf, the Superintendent, insisted that it be staffed twenty-four hours a day, seven days a week. He believed that the public should be able to call on the State Police at any time of day or night. On the weekends, Stockburger would have to prepare meals for the lone Trooper on duty. He would also have to help cater the Colonel's staff meetings. "Colonel Schwarzkopf would hold his staff meetings at the Training School in the mess hall. They would have their dinner first and then the staff meeting would be held afterwards."

Eventually, in June 1929, Stockburger decided to take the State Police entrance exam. Although rumor has it that Schwarzkopf personally asked Stockburger to take the test, this is not true. "I never spoke to the man when I worked in the kitchen and he only shook my hand when I graduated. That was it until much later in my career."

Having passed the test, Stockburger entered the State Police Academy on October 1, 1929 with the 21st Class. It was a fairly large class because the authorized strength of the Department had just been doubled to 480 men. "There wasn't enough room for all of us…so we pitched tents in back of the garage. Where the gymnasium is now was a one-story building that used to store beds – mattresses – because the State had to supply the beds when we were living in the stations. There was a men's room there. So we had to go from the tents to that building to the men's room. At 2:00 or 3:00 in the morning in October and November, that's kind of chilly."

The class graduated on December 31, 1929. Four or five recruits, including Stockburger, were taken to Morristown, which was Troop B Headquarters, and from there a Trooper took Stockburger to his first station assignment: Ramsey Station. It was here where he was assigned for two years. While stationed here in 1930, he was sent to escort Senator Dwight Morrow to a speech he was giving. "I picked him up in Englewood and I took him over to Paterson. It was a rainy day and on the way I hit a trolley track with my motorcycle and I went down. Mr. Morrow told his chauffeur to 'tell that Trooper to ride with us!' but I declined, stating that 'I brought the motorcycle here, I'm going to go back with it.' Mr. Morrow later gave me five dollars and said to 'buy some shoes for the kids!'"

In the 1930s, when the Troopers would pull over someone for speeding, they had to take them to the local Justice of the Peace to pay their fine. Stockburger would tell them to follow him and he would lead them on his motorcycle. "I never had a problem. Everyone always followed me. If we did that today they'd run you over."

One morning while on motorcycle patrol he pulled over a couple from Pennsylvania for speeding. He led them to Louis Shepard, the Justice of the peace in New Brunswick who fined them $10 plus court costs. Stockburger left and when he returned later in the day the couple was still there! The young man, Fred Whal, called Stockburger over and told him that after he left they went out and got a marriage license. They asked the judge to marry them and the judge's wife was going to be a witness. "Would you be my best man?" Caught off guard, Stockburger said, "Why not?" shook his hand and stood in as best man at the impromptu wedding.

Hugo Stockburger worked for many people over his long career, rarely ever having a problem or run-in. "I worked for some good noncoms. I worked for some strict ones. I never had a problem because I did my job. Except one time." A promotion had been announced and Stockburger did not get it. In fact, he could not figure out how the person who got the promotion ever got it and he blamed his sergeant. "I went out on a job and the sergeant called me on the radio and I wouldn't answer him. He called me three times and I wouldn't answer. I was so mad! When I came back to the station he was waiting for me. He took me into the back room and said, 'Look, I know how you feel. But it isn't my fault. I had nothing to do with it. And suppose some Trooper needed some help and you don't answer.' I said, 'Sarge, you're right. I was wrong.' But I sure did get some satisfaction!"

In the early days of State Police, before the implementation of two-way radios, if a station commander needed to contact a Trooper on patrol, a red flag would be displayed during the day (or a special light turned on at night) at gas stations along a Trooper's patrol route. The Trooper then knew to stop and call the station.

On March 1, 1932, Stockburger was on patrol on Route 1 in North Brunswick when he pulled into the Triangle Garage on the corner of Livingston Avenue. The light was on signaling that his station commander needed to speak with him. Charles Lindbergh's baby had just been kidnapped in Hopewell. "My job was to stop all northbound traffic and to see if there was anything unusual."

It would be nearly two-and-a-half years before Bruno Richard Hauptmann would be arrested for the crime. In October 1934 the German immigrant carpenter from the Bronx was extradited to Flemington, New Jersey where he was to stand trial for the kidnapping and murder of the Lindbergh Baby. Hugo Stockburger was assigned to be one of his guards, watching him from noon until 6:00 in the evening.

> My job was to keep him from committing suicide. I sat on one end of the bullpen opposite the outer cell door. Hauptmann would come out of his cell and walk the length of the bullpen. He would walk for hours! I was there to make sure he didn't commit suicide. I didn't wear a tie and I kept my eyes on him at all times so he wouldn't suddenly ram his head into the wall. Hauptmann would never meet me eye to eye. Never! I used to look at him and think to myself, 'You son-of-a-bitch, how can you kill an innocent baby?' How can anyone do that?

One of the reasons Stockburger was given this assignment was because he was fluent in German. It was expected that any time Hauptmann spoke in German, Stockburger would translate the conversation. This simple assignment has grown into an urban legend that Stockburger would speak to Hauptmann directly in German and hopefully get his confession. "Not true," claims Stockburger. "We rarely spoke. Once in a while he wanted to know what the weather was like outside or about ballgames. But he had to start the conversation. I never started it."

Stockburger also sat with Hauptmann at the defense table during the afternoon sessions of the trial:

> I'll never forget the day he jumped up in court. [Special Agent Sisk] was on the witness stand and Hauptmann jumped up, shouting 'That's not true! That's not true!' He surprised me! I was in full uniform. I had a gun on. When I jumped up to grab his shoulder the handle of the gun got caught in the rungs of the chair and it came up and fell over with a crash. Everybody in the courtroom jumped up to see what was going on. It caused a big ruckus. I got him to sit down and told him, 'Look, Richard, that won't help you!'

Hauptmann was found guilty on February 13, 1935 and was sentenced to die in the electric chair. The next day, when he was transferred to the State Prison in Trenton, Stockburger's assignment came to an end.

1935 was a monumental year for Stockburger. On March 13th, in accordance with the Rules and Regulations of the State Police, he submitted his official request to the Superintendent for permission to marry Miss Elizabeth Balough of Mawah, New Jersey. Permission, of course, was granted and on April 8, 1935 they were married. Their son, James, would be born two years later on May 23, 1937.

The following month he received his first promotion when was promoted to rank of Detective. At the end of the month, on May 31st at 11:30 in the morning, Stockburger arrested three men from Belmont, North Carolina, "who had in their possession a Chevrolet coach, that they had stolen on May 30th from the Railroad yards in Charlotte, North Carolina." Then, on June 7th, he arrested two men from New Orleans who had in their possession a .38-caliber revolver and 9 shells. Because of these two arrests, Special Order Number 378 was issued on June 15, 1935 awarding him a "citation for displaying exceptional diligence and observation on the dates of May 31st and June 7th, 1935 in apprehending persons guilty of grand larceny and carrying concealed deadly weapons." By order of the superintendent, he was granted "one day leave of absence in addition to his regular leave."

While the Hauptmann Trial would prove to be the most famous case Stockburger was assigned to, one of the most important and personal cases came about in November 1935. At this time, the Stockburgers were living next door to his good friend, Trooper Warren Yenser and his wife, on Upper Ferry Road in Ewing Township. Sergeant Saltz called Stockburger in the early hours of November 9th, waking him to ask if he was a friend of Trooper Yenser's. He told him he was. "I need you to tell his wife that he just got shot and killed." Stockburger was stunned. He declined to do it and it was the only order he ever questioned.

At 4:45 that morning, Trooper Yenser was on patrol with Trooper J. Matey. They were in pursuit of a stolen Chevrolet Coup in Woodbridge Township. As the troop car pulled along side the stolen car, Trooper Yenser leaned out the passenger side window to blow his whistle. As he did, Edward Metelski shot him point blank in the face with a sawed off shotgun. Trooper Yenser died instantly.

Within two hours of the shooting, Metelski was arrested in Elizabeth, New Jersey and Stockburger escorted him to the jail in New Brunswick. Metelski's girlfriend was later able to slip a gun to him and he escaped from Middlesex County Prison with fellow prisoner Paul Semenkewitz. She was arrested and a massive manhunt for Metelski ensued.

Captain John J. Lamb of the State Police was in charge of the detail to recapture them. According to Stockburger, "we were holding Metelski's girlfriend as a material witness so we arranged a false report that she had been released. Then, we rented a room at Halsey and King Streets in Newark with a good view of the diner where she used to work and we waited." Detectives Long and Stockburger were detailed to the train station in Newark where they were to watch people coming in on trains and buses. Two Newark detectives were supposed to assist Captain Lamb in the apartment across from the diner. For some reason they were unable to make it there so Stockburger and Long were sent instead. "We were there a half hour and I kept looking out the window. I saw two guys coming down the street. It was Metelski and the guy who broke out of prison with him, wearing clothes they had stolen. I knew it was him because I was handcuffed to him when we brought him back from Elizabeth to jail the first time."

As Paul Semenkewitz entered the diner, Metelski continued down the street and around the corner.

I went after him and he had his back to me. I yelled, 'Hey Eddie!' and he turned around. He tried to pull his gun, but it got caught in the pocket of his oversized coat. Before he could get it out, I hit him and we both hit the sidewalk. He immediately surrendered, shouting 'please don't shoot!' A Newark cop and Trooper Long stayed with him while I went after the other guy. I didn't know the other guy except I was told he had a mole on the side of his face. When I went into the diner I saw him sitting there gobbling down a hamburger. He was hungry, I guess. The diner was like a hole-in-the-wall with a long counter and round stools. There were no tables and there were about8 or 10 people inside. When I saw Semenkewitz, I walked up to him and put my gun into his ribs (none to gently) and said, 'if you make a move, I'll pull the trigger!' He surrendered. As escorted him out of the diner, the women behind the counter ran after us, grabbing my arm and shouting 'who's gonna pay for the hamburger??' When she saw the gun, she got quiet and backed away.

Once the men were in custody, Stockburger called the Newark Police captain to say he and Long had captured Metelski and his buddy. The captain, however, had forgotten to change their location assignment from the train station to the diner lookout, so he raced over to the train station. When he got there he found a Trooper and exclaimed, "Where are they? Where are they?" The Trooper had no idea what he was talking about. "Where is *who?*" It then dawned on him that he had made a mistake and he made his way to the diner.

When they got Metelski and Semenkewitz to the Newark Police Station, Stockburger escorted Metelski up the stairs into the station. As he did, he noticed that Metelski would jump every couple of steps. "I looked back and saw a Newark cop kicking him in the ass!" Finally reaching the top, someone suddenly shouted out "COP KILLER!" and it was all over. "I never saw anyone take such a beating." Stockburger reminded the captain that he had to take the prisoners to court the next day. "I thought they were going to kill them!" When Stockburger did get them to court, Metelski's lawyer showed him a picture and asked,

"Is that the man you arrested?"
"Yes, sir."
"Did he look like that?"

"'No sir. He looked like he had a fully loaded gun in his pocket that he was trying to get out.' The attorney never said another word to me."

Edward Metelski was found guilty of the brutal slaying of Trooper Warren Yenser and was executed at Trenton State Prison on August 4, 1936.

A year later, on May 6, 1937 Stockburger was in Lakehurst, New Jersey. It was the day the Zeppelin LZ-129, better known as the *Hindenburg,* was due to arrive from Germany. "I was on duty there. Captain Woodgie sent me down there to help with traffic control." The *Hindenburg* was the pride of Nazi Germany. Longer than three 747s placed end to end, the Zeppelin was a luxury airship filled with highly flammable hydrogen gas. It was originally supposed to be filled with the safer helium gas, but the United States had a military embargo on helium that prevented the Germans from obtaining it. The passengers were the industrial and social elite, as they were the only ones who could afford the $400 tickets during the Great Depression.

As the *Hindenburg* began to dock, it suddenly burst into flames. "I saw the *Hindenburg* explode. The back caught on fire first and it came crashing down. I saw many people jumping to the ground and trying to run away as it came down on top of them. After the explosion it took me 20 minutes to get to a phone. All of the reporters were on the phones calling in their stories. I finally got the call into headquarters. Lieutenant Danny Dunn was in charge then. He wouldn't believe me that it had crashed!" And crash it did.

Of 97 passengers and crew aboard, 36 died, including one of the members of the ground crew. Over in just 32 seconds, the *Hindenburg* disaster signaled the end of the era of luxury airships and was the first crack in the foundation of Hitler's "superior" Nazi Germany.

Stockburger worked on scores of additional cases throughout his career, some noteworthy and many that were routine and he spent most of his career doing detective work. One of his most satisfying cases was that of a series of burglaries in the Princeton, Somerville, Flemington, Hightstown and New Brunswick Station areas. On May 2, 1949 Captain Daniel Dunn, who was now commanding Region "B" (formerly known as "Troop B") submitted a letter of commendation to the State Police Superintendent, Colonel Charles Schoeffel. It "respectfully invited" the Superintendent's attention to the fact that "the persistent questioning and follow-up investigation by Corporal/Detective Stockburger brought about the admission of Stephen J. Shepherd of 17 safe burglaries." One of the items stolen was a movie projector from a school in New Brunswick. The school's PTA and student body had raised the money to buy the projector through bake sales. After Stockburger broke the case, he called the teachers to tell them he had recovered the projector. "I'll never forget the day I called…the teachers nearly flipped with joy! And the children all treated me like a hero." Captain Dunn went a step further and recommended, "that he be granted an extra three days pass."

Stockburger was assigned to many stations during his career. His first assignment, as stated earlier, was the Ramsey Station. From there he was sent in March 1931 to Keyport for three months. In June 1931 he was transferred to the New Brunswick Station where he remained until March 1933. From April 1934 through May 1935 he was assigned to the Princeton Station. This was originally in Penns Neck, just north of Princeton.

When he was designated a Detective in 1935, he was assigned to Troop "C" Headquarters which was located in West Trenton. He went back to New Brunswick in January 1939 where he remained until July 1949

During his second assignment to New Brunswick, he was given two specific investigations. From 1945 to 1946 he was assigned exclusively to the Anthony Puglisi Murder Investigation. Then, from May 1948 to July 1948 he was assigned to a special gambling investigation in Burlington County.

In July 1949, he was promoted to Detective Sergeant and was assigned to the Criminal Investigation Section (CIS) at Division Headquarters in West Trenton. Two years later, on January 1, 1951 Hugo Stockburger was promoted to the rank of Detective First Class. He continued his investigations into such notable cases as the Allentown Bank Robbery (March through August 1951), the Sugarman Murder Investigation (August through October 1951) and the Waterfront Corruption Investigation (November 1951 through December 1952). It was during this last investigation that he was promoted to Lieutenant in September 1952.

It was shortly after being promoted that he worked on the Harold J. Adonis Investigation. This investigation lasted from November 1952 to March 1953. . Harold J. Adonis was the former executive clerk in the office of Governor Alfred E. Driscoll's office from 1943 to 1949. He was under investigation in the state's gambling probe that Stockburger was assigned to, and was one of several former state employees under investigation. He was accused of "…receiving $228,000 to be used in bribing public officials to protect [illegal] gambling" in New Jersey.

> I got the job to check on Adonis. I had to type my reports at home because it was a big secret and they didn't want anybody looking over my shoulder. I was on it two weeks. There was a small article in the Evening News that asked who the former state employee was that was being investigated by the State Police. Adonis read this and took off to Venezuela and from there to Holland. I got a call one afternoon from Captain

Keaten. 'We gotta go to Holland tomorrow morning.' We spent two weeks in Holland trying to get Adonis extradited. The judges came in -- there were six or eight of them --and they wore those white wigs like they did years ago. But we didn't have an agreement to extradite.

While in Holland, Stockburger provided one of four affidavits presented at the extradition hearing. He testified that his investigation had shown that Adonis had spent $43,892 in cash between April 24, 1948 and March 11, 1949 while his state salary at that time was only $4,000. Although Holland would not extradite Adonis, he eventually did return to the United States and was arrested, tried and convicted on charges of tax evasion on $11,869.

A practical man, Stockburger took advantage of his time in Europe. "We were in Holland for two months. Before I came home, I flew to Germany and saw my parents for the first time in thirty years!"

Stockburger was again promoted, on April 7, 1958, to the rank of Captain. The following year, on June 19, 1959, Captain Stockburger and Deputy Attorney General John J. Bergin led a raid on five establishments in Hoboken that were suspected of running illegal gambling operations. Seventeen men, including Hoboken's Housing Authority chairman, were arrested and charged with various gambling offenses.

Another raid under the direct supervision of Stockburger was made in July of that year in North Bergen, New Jersey, resulting in the arrest of five more individuals on gambling charges in what was considered one of Hudson County's biggest gambling raids. Two years later, in July 1961, a raid in Jersey City resulted in the arrest of fourteen men.

The Criminal Investigation Section head, Major D. C. Borchard, retired in 1959 and Stockburger was appointed as his successor and promoted to Major. He served two years in this position until December 28, 1961. It was his birthday and he had reached the compulsory retirement age – 55 years. He spent thirty-three years as a Trooper without ever taking a sick day.

Although his distinguished career with the New Jersey State Police had come to an end, his investigative work did not. In 1962, at the urging of the Attorney General, he accepted an appointment as the Deputy Director of the State Bureau of Alcohol Beverage Control. He retired from this position in 1970 and became Director of Police in his hometown of Milltown.

His final retirement came in 1974 at the age of 62. It was now time to relax with his wife and son, work in his garden and to fish at his shore home in Normandy Beach. He continues to live in the house he built in Milltown in 1939 after his transfer to the New Brunswick Station. Sadly, his wife Elizabeth passed away in 1993.

Reflecting back on his career in the State Police, Stockburger explained that "you have to have a lot of patience, a lot of friends, and a lot of common sense in police work" to be successful. For the rest of his life he remained very loyal to the Superintendent who eventually became his friend, Colonel H. Norman Schwarzkopf. "There is only one superintendent as far as I am concerned. Schwarzkopf."

Major Hugo Stockburger was the oldest living New Jersey State Trooper and the first to ever reach the age of 100. "There is no outfit like the State Police. I'm a State Trooper at heart and I want everybody to know it."

Hugo Stockburger passed away on June 21, 2007. He was buried in Van Liew Cemetery in North Brunswick, New Jersey.

17. The State Police Investigators

The highest-ranking State Trooper among the investigators of the Lindbergh Kidnapping Case was Captain John J. Lamb. Having had prior investigatory experience – he had assisted with the notorious Hall-Mills murder investigation of 1922 among others – he was initially assigned to team-up with Detective Fitzgerald of the Jersey City Police Department.

Captain Lamb was thirty-nine years old when the *Crime of the Century* occurred. Born on Hudson Street in New York City on March 25, 1893 his family moved to Hoboken in 1900. Around the age of 17 he joined the United States Coast Guard and served on the *S. S. Seneca* for one year. He then enlisted in the Army and served with Battery "C" of the 6th Field Artillery from May 3, 1911 until his discharge on August 25, 1915 with the rank of sergeant.

After leaving the army, J. J. Lamb joined the New York City Police in 1916 and then transferred to the New York State Police the following year. While a New York Trooper he attended law school

Once again he attained the rank of sergeant, but he resigned from the State Police in 1919 after just two years on the job. He then went to work with his father at T. Hogan & Sons as a foreman stevedore managing the loading and unloading of ships. He held this job until 1921 when he decided to take the entrance exam for the newly created New Jersey State Police. He passed the test and entered the Academy that September as a member of the first State Police Class.

Because the organization was new and had only five appointed officers, many promotions occurred early on, even while the men were still recruits in training. John Lamb was one of those promoted to Corporal in October

1921. After graduation, he continued to rise quickly through the ranks and, in less than three years, he was promoted to Captain in April 1924.

The Lindbergh investigation began in March 1932 and continued until Hauptmann's arrest in September 1934. During that time promotions, transfers and reassignments continued to occur within the State Police. For example, in June 1932 Lamb was temporarily assigned to command of the State Police training school at Wilburtha.[23] From here he was assigned command of Troop "C."[24]

In August 1935 Captain Lamb was transferred to Department Headquarters in Trenton where he was placed in command of the prestigious Detective Bureau. A few years later, he returned to command Troop "C."

Throughout the 1920s and 1930s, and even into the 1940s the State Police participated in pistol shoot competitions with neighboring State and local police agencies. Captain Lamb was a consistently one of the highest scoring member of the State Police Pistol Team, usually taking second only to Colonel Schwarzkopf. In May 1933 Captain Lamb tied the world record with his 299 score during a pistol match at Wilburtha. He also led the State Police Pistol Team to victory over the 44th Division, New Jersey National Guard and the 78th Division Regular Army.

With the completion of the Lindbergh Case investigation and the conviction and execution of Richard Hauptmann in April 1936, the Superintendent of the New Jersey State Police, Colonel H. Norman Schwarzkopf, awarded Captain Lamb and eight other Troopers the prestigious *Distinguished Service Award,* the highest award granted by the State Police, for their "extraordinary application of duty" and tireless investigative work on the Lindbergh Kidnapping Case.

In 1939 Captain Lamb began to complain to his doctor of discomfort in his stomach. After numerous visits to both his and the State Police's doctor, John Lamb died on June 8, 1940 from *gastric carcinoma* – stomach cancer.

The news of the death of the 47-year-old State Police captain sent shockwaves throughout the law enforcement community. Telegrams and teletypes of condolences flooded into State Police headquarters from around the country. Captain Lamb's funeral was held at St. George's Church in Washington Crossing, New Jersey and he was buried in St. Mary's Cemetery, Trenton. He left behind his widow, Marjorie, and two daughters from his first marriage.

Probably the most well known State Trooper assigned to investigate the Lindbergh Kidnapping was Arthur T. Keaten. "Buster" Keaten, a nickname he took from the famous Hollywood actor, was born in Hoboken, New Jersey on May 20, 1901. He attended grammar school but left in 1916 when he was just 15 years old. In 1920 he took a job with the Western Electric

Company as an installer of telephone switchboards. Then, on September 7, 1922, Buster applied to enter the New Jersey State Police and entered the Academy on October 1st as a member of the 4th Class.

In 1925 Keaten found himself assigned to the Malaga Station in Troop "A." On July 4th of that year, he had a falling out with the Sergeant and Corporal at the Station and he requested a transfer out of Troop "A" to Department Headquarters in Trenton. Instead, he was given a transfer to Troop "A" Headquarters in Hammonton. In August, his superiors wrote, "in view of the attitude taken by Trooper A. T. Keaten 1/c towards the administration of this organization, it is believed that he is not at this time qualified to hold the rank of Trooper First-Class. It is recommended that [he] be reduced…to Trooper." The request was returned, approved, the same day.

This little disciplinary action did little to hinder Keaten's career. In fact, he went on to be one of the most respected investigators in the history of the organization. In February 1927 his request of transfer out of Troop "A" was granted and he was assigned to Department Headquarters in Trenton. On March 1st, he was promoted to the rank of Medical Trooper First-Class and then on December 1st to Medical-Sergeant.

The following year, the State Police was reorganized into a more streamlined organization. Some stations were closed as control and oversight was made more centralized. In addition, the rank structure was revamped and certain ranks were abolished. One such rank to be abolished was Medical-Sergeant and on April 4, 1928 Keaten was reduced back to the rank of Trooper. As this was a result of the reorganization and not a disciplinary action, the next day he was promoted to the rank of Sergeant and assigned to the Central Bureau of Investigation.

On January 31, 1930 Keaten was promoted to Lieutenant and transferred back to Troop "A", although he remained "attached to Headquarters for duty as Assistant Inspecting Officer." He was eventually transferred back to Headquarters on July first.

As the ranking officer in the Detective Bureau in 1932, Lieutenant Keaten became the lead investigator of the Lindbergh Kidnapping Case, a task for which he was awarded the Distinguished Service Award in 1936 by Colonel Schwarzkopf. However, no sooner did Schwarzkopf leave office in June of that year, Lieutenant Keaten was reduced in rank to Sergeant and transferred out of the Detective Bureau to the training school at Wilburtha. This was the same time that Captain Lamb, who had commanded the Detective Bureau since 1935, was also transferred to Wilburtha

This incident requires that we take a slight detour into the background issues that were surrounding the State Police and the Governor in 1936. When the Special Order was issued transferring both Lamb and Keaten to

Wilburtha, it did not explain the motivation behind the move nor behind Keaten's demotion. This is not unusual, as Special Orders, and later Personnel Orders, are issued to make personnel matters official not to offer explanations. That said, State Police lore as well as a New York Times article from July 1936 provide some insight into the events of the summer of 1936.

In June 1936 Governor Harold Hoffman refused to re-appoint Colonel Schwarzkopf to a fourth term as superintendent of the State Police, effectively forcing him to retire. It was well known that Schwarzkopf and Hoffman did not get along and the Governor was eager to get rid of his nemesis at the earliest possible moment. Their animosity dated back to the 1920s when Hoffman was the Commissioner of Motor Vehicles. In those days, the state had Motor Vehicle Inspectors who thought that they were police officers. They would attempt to pull vehicles over to issue summonses for traffic violations. The citizens of the state were confused by this and often complained to Colonel Schwarzkopf, asking if they were legitimate police working on behalf of the State Police. Finally, Schwarzkopf took the matter to the governor who then reprimanded the Motor Vehicle Commissioner – Hoffman.[25]

One of the largest collections housed in the Lindbergh Kidnapping Archive of the New Jersey State Police Museum is the Hoffman Collection, a series of over 20,000 documents generated during the reinvestigation of the Lindbergh Case directed by Hoffman after he came to office in 1936, however there are some documents in the collection that seem to point to Hoffman having an interest in the investigation as far back as March 1932.

While on one hand the Governor believed that Hauptmann did not work alone and was trying to prove this, the investigation also served to deliver a black eye to Colonel Schwarzkopf and the State Police.

When the Lindbergh Case was finally closed and Hauptmann executed in April 1936, Governor Hoffman decided it was time to clean house and purge the State Police of Schwarzkopf and his closest allies, Captain Lamb and Lieutenant Keaten.

A *New York Times* article dated July 16, 1936 further explained that Governor Hoffman forced Schwarzkopf to retire because he felt that the State Police investigation of the Lindbergh Case was "the worst bungled police job in history." He then replaced him with his political ally Colonel Mark O. "Mo" Kimberling, a former State Police major and warden of the State Prison in Trenton. Kimberling was one of the appointed officers brought in personally by Schwarzkopf when he established the State Police in 1921. He served as Adjutant and Deputy Superintendent until 1929 when he allegedly had a falling out with Schwarzkopf and resigned to become warden at the state prison in Rahway. When Hoffman came to power Kimberling was transferred to the state prison in Trenton as warden and given the rank of Colonel ostensibly to rival Schwarzkopf.

Even Major Charles Schoeffel, the deputy superintendent, was not safe from Hoffman's pogrom because he, too, was especially close with Colonel Schwarzkopf.

> Immediately after Colonel Schwarzkopf's retirement, Governor Hoffman appointed Captain Carter as acting superintendent and directed him to demand Major Schoeffel's resignation. Major Schoeffel refused, contending that he was protected by the Veterans' Preference Act of 1928. Later [he] took an 'indefinite' leave of absence."

Schoeffel was allowed to stay and was re-appointed as Deputy by Kimberling who stated, "I decided that he was entitled to a further trial in his position, so I re-appointed him on a temporary basis."

It was probably good that Kimberling was a former trooper, and one with rank. He was actually a very capable leader and once Hoffman was left office after only one term as Governor, Kimberling was then able to come into his own as superintendent.

Keaten's career did recover, but it took some time. It was not until September 1, 1941 that he was promoted back to "acting" Lieutenant and returned to the Detective Bureau. Interestingly, this was just 21 days before Colonel Kimberling retired. The less cynical might interpret it as a *mea culpa* and a wan attempt by Kimberling at trying to make amends. Keaten was made permanent in his rank on October 1, 1941 under the leadership of the new superintendent, Colonel Charles Schoeffel.

On February 23, 1944, Keaten was assigned as Inspector of the Department of State Police. The following year, on April 16th, he assumed the rank of Executive Lieutenant at Headquarters. Two years later, on April 29, 1947 he was promoted to the rank of Captain Inspector. His last promotion came on April 1, 1952 when he was attained the rank of Major and was appointed Executive Officer of the State Police.

Just prior to being promoted to Major, Keaten joined Hugo Stockburger in an investigation of Harold J. Adonis, a former State employee from Governor Driscoll's office who was the subject of a huge investigation for embezzlement and tax evasion. They followed him as he fled to Holland and, although the Dutch would not extradite him, they did finally arrest him when he returned to the United States just a few years later. He was arrested and convicted of tax evasion.[26]

In compliance with the 1949 law that required State Troopers to retire at age 55, Major Keaten retired on May 20, 1956. He lived in the Trenton area until his death in September 1980. In his Last Will and Testament, he requested his cremated remains to be buried "under the yardarm at Division Headquarters" in West Trenton, New Jersey. This was the location of the old Wilburtha Training School where he had spent so much time. "Without much fanfare or ceremony, and with the blessing of [his] widow Lydia," and their children[27] he became the first Trooper to be buried on Stat Police soil.

When the New Jersey State Police Museum and Learning Center opened in October 1992, a memorial garden was established in the courtyard. Major Keaten's ashes were transferred there and on December 15, 1992 he became the first Trooper to interred in the new State Police Memorial Garden.

One of the more controversial State Police investigators of the Lindbergh Case was Lew Bornmann. He was the Trooper who noticed a piece of floorboard missing from Richard Hauptmann's attic – a piece of flooring that wood expert Arthur Koehler later determined was used in the construction of the kidnap ladder. The discovery of this piece of evidence was controversial in its day and it remains so today, as questions of evidence tampering perjury by Bornmann are hotly debated back and forth.

Lewis J. Bornmann was born in Philadelphia, Pennsylvania on May 2nd 1898 or so he thought. He was obviously not immune to controversy and so it should not be surprising that a maelstrom of confusion surrounds even something as simple as his birthday.

In 1926, when he applied to the State Police, he gave 1898 as the year of his birth. This date "was given in all sincerity, it being my belief, then as now, that was the date of my birth." Several years later, when the State Police began using two-way radios, Bornmann applied to the Federal Communications Commission for a radio license. For this he needed to submit his birth certificate however when he tried to obtain a copy, there was no record on file. It had been lost in a fire.

Bornmann then contacted St. Michael's Rectory in Philadelphia for a copy of his Baptismal record. The priest checked their Baptismal Register and found his birthday listed on page 91 as May 2, 1897. Bornmann then submitted this date to the FCC and was granted his license. He then requested to have his personnel record at State Police changed to reflect 1897 as the year of his birth.

This was not a problem until 1951. According to his new birth date, Bornmann was now 54 years old. On July 31, he wrote to Colonel Schoeffel that, "at the time I submitted this record, the compulsory fifty-five year retirement law [enacted in 1949] was not yet in effect, and a year one way or another did not have too much material bearing. At the present time, however, to be held to the 1897 date would mean the loss of a years' work. It is respectfully requested that the date of birth revert back to that given at the time of [my] enlistment as 1898."

The matter was brought to the attention of Robert Peacock[28] in the Office of the Attorney General for a final decision. Peacock stated, "to my mind there is no official record upon which you can rely other than the original application for enlistment." Therefore his year of birth was officially accepted as being 1898.[29]

Lewis Bornmann grew up in Philadelphia and attended two years of high school and two years of night school. In 1915 he moved from Philadelphia to Carney's Point in Salem County, New Jersey. He worked as a millwright on construction sites and as a repairman on pneumatic tools for the DupPont Company just across the bridge in Delaware. He also spent some time as a chauffeur.

A decade later, Bornmann enlisted in the State Police on September 1, 1926 and was assigned to Troop "A" in south Jersey. He was promoted to Corporal and transferred to Troop "C" in the central part of the State in April 1930. On the 20th of that month, Bornmann sent a letter to Colonel Schwarzkopf requesting that his recent promotion be rescinded and that he be returned to the rank of Trooper:

> After careful consideration, I feel that as a Trooper I am in a position to serve the Department better than as a Corporal. It is not that I feel that I am not capable of handling the corporalship, but from my own knowledge of myself I know that as a corporal I would lose all initiative, inasmuch as the duties of that office are very confining.

He also asked not to be transferred out of Troop "A" as "I am engaged to a south Jersey girl, whom with your permission I expect to marry in the very near future." Not surprisingly, the Superintendent disapproved both requests.

The following year, in January 1931, he again asked for a transfer back to Troop "A", but without a request for demotion. This time the transfer was approved, but his stay in Troop "A" did not last very long. On June 2, 1931 he was reduced in rank to Trooper and transferred from Troop "A" to Troop "B" to the Morristown Station. Bornmann was not happy. And neither was the Mayor of Avalon, New Jersey who wrote to the Governor requesting him to help prevent this transfer. He explained that Bornmann was newly married[30] and that his wife was a nurse working in southern New Jersey and could not move away at that time. He was asking for Bornmann to remain attached to Troop "A" as it would "at least permit him to be near his wife."

The Governor took the Mayor's request directly to Schwarzkopf who denied it. He explained that "the orders reducing and transferring Bornmann are part of a disciplinary action against [him] and it would defeat the purposes of discipline to make any change."

Bornmann stayed in Troop "B" until July 1, 1932 when he returned to south Jersey. He was also promoted to the rank of Detective, the rank he carried throughout the rest of the Lindbergh Kidnapping investigation. At the close of that investigation he, too, received the Distinguished Service Award from Colonel Schwarzkopf, one of several accolades for his police work throughout his career.

On June 1, 1942 he was assigned to the Detective Bureau in Trenton and promoted to Detective-Corporal. He eventually attained the rank of Lieutenant in 1951 and his final promotion came on September 1, 1952 when he was made Captain.

Bornmann retired on May 2, 1953 which was either his 55th or 56th birthday. Not much else is known of him, however he did resurface in the mid-1980s when both the BBC and New Jersey Network interviewed him for documentaries they produced about the Lindbergh Kidnapping. During his interviews he recounted the his part of the investigation, the discovery of the matching floorboard as well as a confrontation he had with Governor Hoffmann in Hauptman's attic.

Lew Bornmann died in Absecon, New Jersey, on February 3, 1991.

A flamboyant signature that appears on hundreds of Lindbergh Kidnapping investigation reports in the State Police files is that of Sergeant Andrew Zapolsky. He worked diligently not only on the Lindbergh Case, for which he received the Distinguished Service Award, but also on dozens of other investigations that brought in several letters of praise from outside agencies. One commendation came from within the Department of State Police. On May 26, 1931 Special Order 155 was issued in which it was stated that

> The Detective Bureau of the New Jersey State Police is hereby commended for the apprehension of *Anthony Alessia* and particular commendation is given to Lt. A. T. Keaten and Sgt. Andrew Zapolsky for the diligence and persistency, which they have displayed, and for the comprehensive and effective manner in which they have followed their purpose. In recognition of their accomplishment, two weeks

additional leave with pay is granted to Lt. A. T. Keaten and
Sgt. Andrew Zapolsky.

Just a year earlier Zapolsky had to miss rifle practice because he was tied up
with an active investigation. His supervisor wrote to Colonel Schwarzkopf,

> Detective Andrew Zapolsky has been working on the *Jack
> Buckles* murder case and has obtained some excellent leads,
> which show a good possibility of revealing the murderer.
> The chances of reaching a successful solution of the murder
> might be greatly impaired should Det[ective] Zapolsky be
> removed from the case at this time.

It was not just famous kidnappings and murders that Zapolsky investigated.
For example, he helped capture the bandits who robbed the Farmers National
Bank in Deposit, New York in 1935 after it was discovered that they had
crossed state lines into New Jersey. He also helped to investigate the theft of
copper plates that had been stolen from the Panelyte Corporation. No crime
was to insignificant to be investigated so it was Zapolsky who assisted in
the successful investigation of stolen Johnson & Johnson toothbrushes from
various trade outlets throughout New Jersey.

Andrew Zapolsky began his State Police career on August 15, 1927. He
brought with him some interesting prior work experience. From August 1920
to May 1923 he had served as a Pennsylvania State Police Officer. He left
the State Police when he "entered in grocery business for myself" and from
March 1923 until June 1924 he ran a grocery store. From June 1924 until his
enlistment he worked as a coal miner in the Pennsylvania coalmines.

Prior to enlisting in the New Jersey State Police, Zapolsky lived in
Shenadoah, Pennsylvania. He had come to this country from *Wilno*, Poland
where he was born on September 14, 1897. After the turn of the century,
newly independent Lithuania claimed *Wilno* as its historic capital. Today, the
town of *Wilno* is known as by its Lithuanian name, *Vilnius* and it continues
to serve as the capital of Lithuania.

He was a World War I veteran having served in the United States Army
in the 103rd Infantry for two years from September 20, 1917 until May 20,
1919. A few years after the war, on June 6, 1923, he married Anna and a year
later their sun Edward was born on April 7th.

After enlisting in the New Jersey State Police, Zapolsky moved his family
to Hamilton Township, New Jersey where they lived until they moved into
the city of Trenton taking up residence in a house on Chambers Street.

Zapolsky showed he had good detective skills and just two years after enlisting, on October 1, 1929 he was designated a Detective and stationed at Troop "A" Headquarters in Hammonton. Just two years after this, he was promoted to Corporal and assigned to Department Headquarters on February 27, 1931. Just three months later, on May 26th, he was promoted to Sergeant and then Detective Sergeant.

He remained a Detective Sergeant for many years, and it was not until July 1, 1947 that he was promoted to Detective 1/c. He was eventually assigned to the Criminal Investigation Section and on February 19, 1951 he was promoted to Lieutenant. The following year, on April 1, 1952, he reached the rank of Captain. Just four months later, on August 16, 1952 Captain Andrew Zapolsky retired having served 25 years in the Outfit.

Zapolsky's illustrious career nearly came to an end before it even got started thanks to a bad accident he had with his troop car. On the evening of February 14, 1929 he and Corporal Reilly were injured in the line of duty when they were involved in an auto accident: the Troop Car collided with a freight train while on patrol during a snowstorm at Goshen, Cape May. Reilly was slightly injured but the accident resulted in Zapolsky suffering from serious head, face, neck, chest and shoulder injuries, a fractured nose and he nearly lost his left eye. He was granted a month's sick leave with pay to recover from his injuries in March 1929. These injuries plagued him for the rest of his life, causing among other ailments, arthritis in his shoulders and frequent severe headaches.

By the time he retired, he had become very anxious about his health. In 1952 he wrote, "I have been under continuous care of doctors since the accident and will have to continue to do so indefinitely." In July of the same year he wrote that "since the accident, there are some particles of glass remaining in the flesh in close proximity of the eyes, and every couple of years, a piece of it works its way to the surface and requires the service of a physician to remove it."

Zapolsky and Reilly both survived the crash and went on to full State Police careers, Reilly retiring in 1945 as a Sergeant. Even after Zapolsky retired, he continued to suffer from the injuries he received over twenty years earlier. He enjoyed seventeen years of retirement, before he died on June 18, 1969.

Samuel J. "Sammy" Leon was another prominent investigator of the Lindbergh Case. He spent a lot of time with Joseph Perrone, the taxi driver who received a ransom note to deliver to the go-between, Doctor Condon. So much time that Perrone took to writing him notes that began, "Dear Zappy."

Sammy Leon was born in Perth Amboy, New Jersey on March 13, 1904. Like most of the Troopers of his era, he only attended grammar school up to 8th grade. He was a laborer on the Pennsylvania Rail Road at Trenton. He enlisted in the Marine Corps on October 14, 1922 and served with honor until his discharge on October 24, 1925. He was a Private First Class and was sent to Nicaragua as part of the "American intervention" that attempted to stabilize the country. After his discharge he returned to the Pennsylvania Rail Road, this time working in Plainsboro.

Leon was twenty-three years old when he enlisted in the State Police as a member of the 13th State Police Class. He was a classmate of Lewis Bornmann and when they graduated, he was assigned to Troop "B" Headquarters in Morristown, where he stayed until March 1927. At that time he was briefly stationed at Columbus Station but by August 1927 he was back at Morristown, this time in charge of the Detective Bureau, where he remained until May 1947.

After serving in Flemington and Somerville Stations from 1947 through 1951, he was eventually detached to the Criminal Investigation Section (C. I. S.) at Division Headquarters in West Trenton in July 1951. He was permanently assigned there two years later on January 20, 1953.[31]

One of the first Detectives in the State Police, Leon was involved in a dozen murder and robbery investigations, including the murder of small time mobster Willie Moretti of Newark under the direction of fellow Trooper Nuncio DeGaetano. A year before his involvement in the Lindbergh Case,[32] he was a key figure in the apprehension of Edward Kettering. Kettering had murdered Charles Cavanaugh, the Chief of Police of Bernardsville, New Jersey, on Labor Day, 1931. "There were scores of suspects and speculation on who killed the chief, ranging from jealous lovers to bootleggers to the chief's own brother."

Because of his investigative skills, he was assigned in 1941 to the "newly created United States Un-American Activities Committee and commissioned as a Special Agent of the United States Congress." The House Committee on Un-American Activities was also known as the *Dies Committee* after Republican Congressman Martin Dies, Jr. of Texas, who co-founded and co-chaired the committee in 1938. The committee investigated German-American connections to the Nazi Party as well as the Ku Klux Klan as well as some potential Communist activities in the country.[33]

Sammy Leon and his first wife, Jean, had a son who was born in 1930. Samuel J. Leon, Jr. followed in his father's footsteps and became a New Jersey State Trooper in 1954. He and Jean were eventually divorced and on February 9, 1953 he married Lillian Morecraft.

After 31 years of service, he retired from the State Police on March 13, 1958 as a Detective Second Class and in 1963 he and his wife moved to Bound Brook, New Jersey. On June 9, 1985 Samuel Leon died at the Somerset Medical Center in Somerville, New Jersey at the age of 81.

Eugene A. Haussling was one of the few early investigators to have completed high school. Born on February 25, 1896 in Newark, New Jersey he attended school locally. He spent three years at the East Side High School and finished his last year at Central High School taking night classes. He then went on to take business courses at Merchants' & Bankers' Business College for a year.

In 1917 Gene Haussling started off his working career as an office manager at the National Liberty Insurance Company in Newark.[34] On December 17, 1917 he enlisted in the United States Army Coast Artillery at Fort Howard, Maryland and served during the First World War as a Sergeant and First Class Gunner until March 19, 1919. When he was discharged he returned to the New York office of the National Liberty Insurance Company. The following year, he took a position as office manager at the Joseph M. Brennan & Company in Newark. He finished his pre-State Police career working from 1921 to 1922 in the Essex Building in Newark.

Haussling was 27 years old when he enlisted in 1923. In those days, Troopers were not making very much money and they were required to live in the barracks with only three days off each month. So, with his prior business experience it should not be too surprising that on September 30, 1924, he resigned from the State Police so that he could re-enter the insurance business. It did not work out as well as he would have liked, so he wrote to the superintendent asking to return to the State Police. His request was granted and he was reinstated as a Trooper on September 1, 1925. It would be another twenty-seven years before he would leave the State Police again.

Haussling was one of the four original State Police Detectives and was assigned to the newly created Detective Bureau on October 1, 1929. He was another one of the recipients of the Distinguished Service Award for his work on the Lindbergh Kidnapping investigation where he was assigned to check on the northern New Jersey angles of the case.

A year after the Hauptmann Trial, he worked with Sam Leon on the Emile Cota murder case in Hamilton Township, New Jersey. "After other investigators had questioned the woman's husband, Ramon, Haussling rearrested him and finally obtained a confession."

Throughout the 1920s Haussling was promoted to various ranks ranging from Clerk and Medical Trooper 1/c to Sergeant and eventually Detective. For a short time, from April 1, 1930 to July 1, 1930 he was relieved as detective and assigned to command the Columbus Station. It was not until February 15, 1943 that Haussling was promoted again, this time to the rank of Lieutenant-Detective and he held that rank until he retired, on February 24, 1951, his 55th birthday.

Eugene Haussling died suddenly at 4 PM on March 21, 1970 of an apparent heart attack. He was driving his new Dodge sedan on Stonyhill Road in Eatontown, New Jersey just down the road from their home. He slumped over the steering wheel and the car continued out of control until it came to a stop after jumping the curb a short distance away. Fortunately the car was going slowly and there was no damage to the car and his wife Edith, who was a passenger, suffered no injuries. His funeral was held a few days later and he is buried in Fairmont Cemetery in Newark, New Jersey.

Joseph Wolf of the Lambertville State Police station had just four years in the outfit when the call came that Lindbergh's child had been kidnapped. The twenty-eight year old corporal who stood just over six feet tall was the first State Trooper on the scene and filed the Major Initial Report that began the massive investigation that earned him the Distinguished Service Award in 1936.

Joe was stationed in Lambertville in 1931, a year after being assigned to the New Egypt station. Prior to his assignment there, on March 30th, he was placed in command of the Alpine Station just outside Englewood, New Jersey having been promoted to Corporal just 25 days earlier.

He originally came from Paterson, New Jersey, where he was born on April 4, 1903. He and his wife, the former Ethel Smith, later lived in Morristown with their daughter Arleen. He left school after the 8th Grade and in March 1918 went to work for the American Railway Express Company in Paterson as a clerk and platform worker. He held this position until July 1927 when he took a job with the Hearne Baking Company in Morristown where he earned between $160 and $200 a month. A year later, on March 15, 1928, he enlisted in the State Police.

When Joe Wolf graduated from the Academy, he was assigned to Troop "C" in central New Jersey. He remained assigned to the Lambertville station throughout the course of the Lindbergh investigation, until September 7, 1935 when he was made Assistant and later Station Commander at Scotch Plains. Once the Blairstown Station opened he became the Station Commander there.

Corporal Wolf was forced to take a demotion back to Trooper on July 1, 1932. Special Order 125 reduced the rank of thirty-two troopers due to the "Economy Program of 1932"; in other words the Great Depression. He was promoted back to Corporal in September 1935 just prior to taking command of Scotch Plains.

On October 28, 1941 Captain Daniel Dunn wrote a letter to Colonel Schoeffel in which he recommended a promotion for Corporal Wolf. He also explained to the Colonel that

> Since being located in that area [Blairstown] he has endeavored to put the State Police program over to the citizens of that section and enjoys their respect as well as that of the enforcement authorities.

The Colonel concurred with Dunn's recommendation and promoted Wolf to Sergeant on December 1, 1941. He was eventually promoted to Lieutenant in July 1949 and was made the Executive Officer of Troop "B." When he was promoted to Captain in July 1953, he was sent to Troop "D" as the Commanding Officer overseeing the newly opened New Jersey Turnpike.

In addition to his commendation for his work on the Lindbergh investigation, he was also cited for an incident in 1935 in Passaic County. Trooper Joe Wolf assisted with a raid on the "gangers bungalow" in the early morning hours of Sunday June 23rd when he and his fellow Troopers, "fully cognizant of the peril of their task, courageously carried out their respective assignment and effected the capture of [the] suspects without firing a shot."

He received yet another citation in 1949 when now Lieutenant Wolf helped to solve a series of gasoline station hold-ups and robberies that had occurred throughout the northern part of the state.

Captain Joe Wolf retired from the State Police on April 4, 1958 after 30 years service. He and his wife eventually moved to Basking Ridge, New Jersey where he died on November 12, 1987.

Corporal William Frederick Horn is most known for being the Trooper who interrogated Cecilia Barr about the Lindbergh ransom money she received while working at the Loew's Sheridan Theater on November 26, 1933. He, along with John Wallace, was one of Arthur Keaten's top aids working on the kidnapping's New York angle.

Horn was very familiar with New York City, having been born there on May 13, 1898 and his father still lived in Brooklyn in the 1930s. His parents were German immigrants and he himself spoke the language.

William Horn was a veteran of the First World War having served in the United States Navy from April 6, 1918 to July 25, 1919 as a Quartermaster 2nd Class.

Prior to enlisting in the State Police on March 16, 1927, Horn held a variety of jobs. Beginning in February 1922 he worked as the manager of a restaurant. When he left that job in March 1925, he went to work as a railroad car inspector for a year. "For the past nine months and at the present time I am employed as a motorcycle patrolman in the township of Teaneck" where he had been living for the past six years. Although he was on the force for a short time (April 15, 1926 to February 23, 1927), he was considered a very good police officer with a good reputation. He was someone who was very well thought of in town.

On September 19, 1929 Horn resigned from the State Police to accept an appointment with the Bergen County Traffic Police. This job was not to his liking and, just as Eugene Haussling had done just four years earlier, Horn sent a handwritten letter to Colonel Schwarzkopf asking to be reinstated in the State Police. The letter was sent on December 27, 1929 and was brought before an Officers' Meeting where his request was approved. He was told to report for a required medical examination and then to report for duty on January 16, 1930. He was re-enlisted as a Trooper and assigned to the Freehold Station in Troop "C."

On September 5, 1935 Corporal-Detective Horn was assigned to the Detective Bureau in Trenton. He was later promoted to Sergeant in 1924 and on July 1, 1947 he was promoted to Detective 1/c. He retired two years later on October 1, 1949.

William Horn and his wife, Charlotte, moved from their home in Red Bank to Asbury Park in 1963 and then to Belmawr the following year. They eventually ended up in the elite town of Rumson where he died on September 30, 1989 at the age of 91.

One of the Troopers that were present with Lieutenant Keaten and the New York City Policemen when Richard Hauptmann was arrested on September 19, 1934 was John B. "Jack" Wallace, Jr.

Jack Wallace has an interesting and active background. "He made an outstanding record as an investigator and was responsible for the successful completion of many criminal cases. He was born in the town of Clifton, New Jersey on August 15, 1901. He attended grammar school and then night school. Prior to joining the State Police, he was an expert silk weaver working for the Henry Doherty Silk Company in Clifton, New Jersey. He held this position from 1916 to 1924.

He was very active in sports and represented the silk mill on their baseball, soccer and basketball teams. He even had a little experience with a racing horse when he was growing up that bellowed to his father.

Wallace entered the State Police Academy on April 1, 1924 and graduated on June 30th. Two years later, in July 1926, George W. Mair of Clifton, New Jersey sold his feed store as well as his additional business in Patterson, to Wallace's father. Trooper Wallace requested a six-month leave of absence beginning in August "for the reason that my father wishes me to take over the management of his newly purchased business." This request was immediately denied so Wallace resigned on August 1st. Two months later he was back, being reinstated on October 20th.

Wallace was promoted to Sergeant on January 1, 1929. At the end of the year, on December 1st, Wallace did receive a leave of absence (without pay) but it was not to manage a feed store. Rather, he was hired to reorganize the Hackensack Police Department.

> Sergeant John Wallace of the Flemington Sub-Station of the New Jersey State Police [was] recently given a nine months leave of absence to instruct the Hackensack Police. [He] will take up his duties [on] December 1, [1929]. He will be known as the acting chief and the city will pay his salary.

The Mayor of Hackensack, Herman van der Wart said, "this is a new idea, I believe, and my own…Sergeant Wallace will stay here until such time as we can select a man for the job of chief." And it was a successful idea.

> Wallace had two things in his favor – an expert training in police work and a reputation of complete honesty. The general morale of the [Hackensack] department has been improved. New, modern systems have been installed; much of the petty jealousy has been removed. Wallace has done his job well.

When John Wallace returned from his leave of absence in the summer of 1930, he was promoted to Lieutenant. Unfortunately he was one of the thirty-two State Troopers affected by the cutbacks during the Great Depression and he was reduced to Sergeant-Detective in July 1932. He regained his rank in July 1936.

In April 1946 he was assigned to Troop "C" as the Executive Lieutenant and later, in 1949, as Captain.

While John Wallace did not receive the Distinguished Service Award, he did get the Department of Merit Award for his "comprehensive and productive co-operation," and assistance rendered to the investigators of the Lindbergh Kidnapping Case. He also was cited and commended by

Special Order on July 26, 1934 for "exceptional and meritorious service" for arresting and securing the conviction of James Duncan, Walter Bennett and Donald Tremper for the murder of Michael Dries. Wallace investigated the case between August 1, 1933 and July 17, 1934 and displayed "ingenuity, sound judgment and perseverance" in the case. He was also granted an extra three-days leave of absence.

John Wallace was married three times. We know this because of an interesting clause that Colonel Schwarzkopf included in the rules and regulations of the State Police when he founded the organization in 1921. If you were single when you enlisted in the State Police but later wished to marry, you first had to submit a request for permission from the Superintendent. It harkened back to Schwarzkopf's time in the military and this quirk remained on the books until the 1960s. This was really a formality, but it was required. So, on June 11, 1926 Wallace submitted a request to marry Marion Akers of Lambertville. Later, on July 27, 1934 he submitted a request to marry Loretta A. Henry of Trenton. Finally, he requested to marry Evelyn Wood of Long Island, New York on July 11, 1942. All of the requests were approved. [35]

Captain John Wallace retired from the State Police as the Traffic Officer in 1952. He and his wife moved to Ft. Meyers Beach, Florida where they lived until April 1967 when they returned to New Jersey. He remained very active in the Former Trooper Association and was heavily involved with their Education Fund. In 1971 he served on the Banquet Committee that helped plan the State Police's 50th Anniversary banquet that was held in Atlantic City on October 2 of that year.

John Wallace died in Lakewood, New Jersey in September 1985.

Another Trooper who received the Distinguished Service Award for his work on the Lindbergh Case was Nuncio T. "Nick" DeGaetano. His parents were Italian immigrants and spoke little English so Nick grew up bi-lingual, speaking Italian fluently. He was born on August 25, 1905 in Miami, Florida and attended grammar school and three years of high school in Jacksonville. The family moved to Newark in June 1927 where he worked as a brick mason until November 15, 1928 when he became a doorman at the Branford Theater on Market Street in Newark.

On August 15, 1921 Nuncio DeGaetano enlisted in the 124th Infantry of the Florida National Guard. He remained with them until June 12, 1927 when he moved to New Jersey. On June 27th, he enlisted with the 102nd Cavalry of the New Jersey National Guard and remained with them until September 18, 1928.

The following year, he applied to the New Jersey State Police and was enlisted on March 16, 1929. His father was very glad to learn that his son had passed his entrance exam and he supported his decision to join the State Police. His mother, while glad that her son passed the exam, did not want him to enlist. She said that he was her only son and she did not want him away from home.

Nick DeGaetano was a very good investigator, a fact that his superiors recognized early on in his career. On April 1, 1931, with just two years in the outfit, he was promoted to Detective. Later that year, because of a transfer to Troop "B", he was returned to the rank of Trooper but on July 1, 1932 he was designated a detective once again.

He spent most of his career as a detective, being promoted to Detective-Corporal and then, in July 1947 to Detective 2/c. He was quickly promoted to Detective 1/c and on March 23, 1952 he was promoted to Lieutenant. Less than a year later, on July 1, 1953 he attained the rank of Captain, something that would have made his mother very proud.

When the Lindbergh kidnapping occurred in 1932, DeGaetano was one of the first to arrive at the Lindbergh estate on the night of March 1st. It was he who discovered the footprints under the nursery window and the kidnap ladder lying near the tree line a several yards away from the house.

In addition to appearing to testify, Nuncio DeGaetano was also assigned with other Troopers to duty at the Flemington Court House during the Hauptmann Trial. On January 25, 1935 he arrived at 10:00 in the morning and entered the Court House through the Warden's office. This was the only means of entrance and exit used by the Troopers and other police officers assigned to the trial.

Captain Lamb met him there and immediately sent him out to purchase meal tickets at the local Methodist Episcopal Church in town. When DeGaetano returned to the Court House, Assistant Attorney General Robert Peacock requested him to have a prescription filled at the drug store "and to return with the medicine as soon as possible."

DeGaetano ran the errand for Peacock but this time, when he returned with the medicine, he ran into Lieutenant Dineen, Sergeant Grafenecker and Detective Cashmen of the New York City Police outside the Warden's office. They were there to testify on behalf of the State that day. They told DeGaetano that the door was locked and that they could not get into the office. Seeing a couple of police officers inside the office, DeGaetano tried, unsuccessfully, to get their attention by knocking on the door. When this failed, he and the other officers decided to walk around to the front of the Warden's office and use the door there. "Upon arriving at the front door, Warden McCrea bolted the door as I attempted to open it."

DeGaetano assumed that the warden did not recognize him so he announced that he was a member of the New Jersey State Police. He also showed the subpoena that was issued to him regarding his court appearance. When the Warden continued to ignore him he added that he was carrying medicine for Assistant Attorney General Peacock and that he was waiting for him to deliver it. "To this the warden stated, 'I am letting no son-of-a-bitch in!' and in turn [I] stated 'you come out here and call me a son-of-a-bitch and I'll poke you in the nose!'" DeGaetano stood there for a moment and finally caught the attention of Corporal Horn who was inside near the Warden. He tried to give the medicine to Horn so he could pass it along to Peacock but the Warden "absolutely refused to open the door."

So, he walked back around to the side door and lo and behold, the Warden was already there, again refusing to open the door. "Rather than enter into any further controversy, [I] proceeded to the front entrance of the Court House and remained there until the noon recess…[when I] gave Mr. Peacock his medicine in front of the Court House and informed him of the above occurrence."

The Warden did not file an official complaint against Detective DeGaetano and no explanation was ever given for the Warden's bizarre behavior.

Twenty years after the Lindbergh investigation, DeGaetano was involved in another high profile case – the Willie Moretti murder. Willie Moretti was a low-level mafia strongman and racketeering partner of Longy Zwillman. His base of operations was Bergen County, specifically Newark. "Besides contract murders, extortion schemes and illegal gambling, Moretti was heavily involved with narcotics trafficking, and he often worked in cooperation with New York mobsters Lucky Luciano, Joe Adonis and…Frank Costello."

By the late 1940s Moretti's mental health had begun to deteriorate. "He became delusional and 4extraordinarily talkative…and his fellow mobsters worried about what he might say to the wrong people." After being called before the Senate's Kefauver Committee that was investigating organized crime Moretti was seen as a potential threat and on October 4, 1951 he was gunned down in Joe's Elbow Room in Cliffside Park, New Jersey.

The investigation was not an easy one and remains unsolved. According to Leo Coakley's *Jersey Troopers*, "The state probe continued for three years. It ended in controversy, with the politicians hurling charges in legislative inquiries, and the troopers involved finding themselves in the familiar role of 'man-in-the-middle.'"

The investigation did have some benefits in that it led to the shutting of illegal casinos and the arrests of Joe Adonis, Frank Erickson and Sol Moretti "all men of stature in the hierarchy of the metropolitan area syndicate." It also led to the expansion of the role of the State Police in the probes of organized crime.

A year after the Moretti investigation ended, Nick DeGaetano suffered a massive heart attack while on vacation with his wife Edythe and died on July 4, 1955. He was still on active duty and was just five years away from his retirement. He is buried in St. Peter's Cemetery in New Brunswick, New Jersey.

The New Jersey State Troopers who were assigned to investigate the Lindbergh Case in addition to their other duties generated a quarter of a million pages of reports in just over two-and-a-half years. But as evidenced in their biographical snapshots above, the Lindbergh Case was just one event in their long careers of service to the citizens and State of New Jersey.

18. William Allen

No one would ever have heard of William Allen had it not been for a "call of nature." Had the African American truck driver not pulled over on the side of the Hopewell-Princeton road that spring afternoon and ducked into the woods to relieve himself his name could have been lost to history and the Lindbergh Baby may never have been found. For it was William Allen that serendipitously discovered the remains of Charles Lindbergh, Jr., just five miles from the Lindbergh Estate on May 12, 1932.

The story is recounted in just about all of the books written about the case and even school children know the tale of discovery; many even remember William Allen's name. But very few people, other than his family, know anything else about him. Even his obituary – which ran in the New York Times – mentions nothing about him other than his connection to the Lindbergh Case.

William Allen was a very hard working and quiet man who was deeply loved by his wife, the former Helen B. Jennings and their children. He wore a small neatly trimmed mustache and "smoked cheap five cent cigars with yellow bands on them." He was the type of person who would do just about anything for anyone.

> No matter what the weather was – snow, rain or hail, my father was there to take anyone in [town] to the store or to the doctor. He was a Jack-of-all-trades and master of none. That was my father. He touched everyone's heart no matter what race, religion, rich or poor. He was there.

Allen was born in Buckingham County, Virginia in September 19, 1889 to Tempy Allen. [36] There is some question as to whether his birthday is on the 19th or actually on the 1st. However, according to his youngest daughter, Elinor, "my father swore that he was born on September 19th, so we always celebrated his birthday on that date." That is also the date cited by the Social Security Death Database.

In 1900, when he was just eleven years old, he left Virginia and moved north to find work and to be near his sister who lived in Philadelphia. He held several jobs as both truck driver and laborer including the Keystone/Barbour Steel Company; W. R. Cleveland contractors; W. G. Runkles of Trenton and William Titus of Hopewell.

He also worked on the construction of the Pulaski Skyway as a laborer. Construction on the skyway began in 1930, which was plagued by 15 fatal accidents. William Allen almost contributed to number 16: "He fell several feet to the ground sustaining serious injuries. He was transported to the hospital in Freehold, New Jersey" where he eventually recovered.

Allen was working for William Titus when he discovered the Lindbergh Baby. He was hired on October 1, 1925 and on May 12, 1932 he and fellow employee Orville Wilson were hauling a truckload of timber through the Mount Rose section of Hopewell. They were following their boss's son, Livingston Titus, from Princeton to the "old saw mill on the old turnpike on the Woodsville-Hopewell Road." Allen himself described the scene to a *New York* Times reporter in 1935:

> We came from Princeton with a load of timber. About half
> a mile from Hopewell I stop the truck and walk into the
> woods. After I went in I seen the skeleton through a bush. I
> went through the bush. There is a body in a shallow trench.
> So I call Mr. Wilson in the truck. 'Whatsa matter?' he say.
> I say 'Looka here. Don't know about anybody losing a child
> except Colonel Lindbergh. Let's get out of here!'

They drove into Hopewell looking for Charlie Williamson, one of the local policemen that he knew. "We stopped at Hopewell, and after looking around for Charlie found him in the barber shop. I said, 'could you talk to me for a couple of minutes?' He said sure, he'd talk to me for five if I wanted to." Allen explained what he had stumbled upon in the woods.

> [Charlie Williamson] took me back to the truck and after
> I delivered the load of blocks I had on the truck I took him
> to the road where we found the baby. The baby was about

forty-five feet back from the road. After I sowed to Charlie
he went and got some State policemen and I drove my truck
back home and went to dinner. After I got home Williamson
and some plainclothesmen came and got me and took me to
Lindbergh's house.

William Allen had indeed discovered the Lindbergh Case and secured
a place for himself in the annals of history. More importantly he provided
closure for Charles and Anne Lindbergh. When Allen was taken to the
Lindbergh estate to give his official statement to the police, the Lindberghs
snubbed him. His son, William Allen, Jr. was in awe when he learned that his
father had gone to Lindbergh's home. "What did he say to you, pop?" "Not
a damn thing. Not 'thank you', not 'kiss my ass, *nothing.*" The Lindberghs
refused to speak to him.

To make matters worse, when it came time to issue reward money to
those who had provided evidence leading to the conviction of the Lindbergh
baby's murderer, William Allen was not on the list! He had even testified at
Hauptmann's trial. Finally, Governor Hoffman was convinced that he was
indeed entitled to his fare share of the $25,000 reward and in 1938 the State
of New Jersey gave him $5,000.

Allen was embarrassed by all of the attention he received. The day after
the discovery both he and Orville Wilson appeared at the home of William
Titus, their employer. "Both were plainly embarrassed when they strolled
into the yard at Marshall's Corner, about three miles from Hopewell, to find
themselves facing a battery of cameras. William Allen…finally posed for the
newsreel and repeated three or four times the simple tale of his discovery of
the body."

The New Jersey State Legislature also formally commended Mr. Allen
for his behavior at the time of the discovery because he had "cautioned
Orville Wilson…not to touch the body, and had promptly notified the local
police."

Unfortunately it was not long after his fifteen minutes of fame that the
real life returned and, due to the economic hardships caused by the Great
Depression Mr. Titus was forced to lay off William Allen. That is when
those who were eager to exploit anyone and anything for profit pounced.
Promoters of a side show tried to take advantage of Allen and the tragedy he
discovered.

They persuaded him to appear on tour with a circus [and]
when that was barred by the State of Massachusetts they put
him in a Coney Island exhibit, charging the public 10 cents

to see him in a curtained booth. Governor A. Harry Moore of New Jersey learned of it and protested to the New York Police…[who] succeeded in persuading the shows promoters to close it.

Three cities in Massachusetts had banned the circus act and Mayors Horace Baker of Brocton and Thomas McGrath of Quincy "characterized the Negro's proposed appearance in their cities as 'contemptible commercialism.'"

Realizing that it was not really William Allen who was trying to exploit the gruesome discovery, "a group of citizens called on the Governor to give Allen a job and a handyman's post at the New Jersey Home for Girls was found for him."

William Allen continued working until his retirement sometime in the 1950s and he continued to live in the Trenton area. On the morning of December 20, 1965 he drove his daughter Elizabeth to work. He was supposed to call his doctor when he got home to set up an appointment "but instead his appointment was with God." William Allen died in his home at the age of 76.

19. *Violet Sharp*

During the course of the investigation of the Lindberg kidnapping, the police interrogated the domestic servants working for both the Lindberghs and Mrs. Lindbergh's mother, Elizabeth Morrow. Violet Sharp[37] was an English maid come waitress working in the Morrow household in Englewood, New Jersey. She got the $85 a month job on May 13, 1930 through the Richard T. Hutchinson Bureau for Domestic Help of Madison Avenue, New York.

Violet was very popular among the other servants and it was alleged that she was engaged to, or at least very friendly with, the butler, Septimus Banks. According to a June 12, 1933 interview with Mrs. Katherine Cornels who knew Violet, "her only intimate friend was Banks the Butler at the Morrow home who Violet [said] had proposed marriage to her on several occasions and that she was undecided as to whether to accept or not." [38]

When it came time for the police to question Violet, they noticed her suspicious behavior. It quickly became obvious to them that she was lying about her whereabouts on the night of the kidnapping. The police questioned her on three separate occasions and each time Violet would contradict her previous statements. On June 10, 1932 the police called again, requesting a fourth interview. She agreed but before they arrived she had run up to her bedroom and drank silver polish. It contained cyanide. She staggered down the servants' stairs to the pantry where she collapsed and died moments later.

Violet Sharp's suicide convinced the press and initially the police that she was indeed somehow involved with the kidnapping. Further investigation, however, failed to implicate her in the crime yet she remains a person of interest for many researchers because of her contradictory statements and mysterious suicide.

Violet's death became an international scandal. The *Daily Mirror* in England ran the headline: "Murder By Third Degree." Colonel Schwarzkopf received a telegram from Leslie Randall, a correspondent with the *Daily Express* stating that "English newspapers [are] greatly concerned over what appears [to] them [to] be premature conclusion of police [that] Violet Sharpe [sic] had guilty knowledge [of the] kidnapping…Newspapers (but not Daily Express) is suggesting Sharpe [sic] may have committed suicide because [she was] terrorized by third degree methods."

On June 20, 1932 Brigadier General Clifton Brown, a Conservative Member of Parliament from Newbury rose in the House of Commons to address the issue of possible mistreatment of a British subject by the New Jersey State Police.

> *Is my Honourable Friend aware that the parents, owing to letters that they have had from their late daughter, are quite convinced that, owing to the methods of investigation that have been pursued, she committed suicide and that they are very anxious in the interests of justice that the whole case should be investigated?*

G. Shepherd, the acting British Consul General in New York was instructed by London to investigate the suicide and the role played by the State Police. He contacted Governor Moore of New Jersey and arranged a meeting with Inspector Walsh, Lieutenant Keaten as well as with the Governor in order to examine any and all documentation pertaining to the Sharp investigation.

The Governor helped as much as he could but he also made it clear that "he would stand 'squarely behind' Colonel H. Norman Schwarzkopf in the investigation of suspects in the Lindbergh kidnapping." In response to criticism by Emerson L. Richards, the Republican Floor Leader in Washington, DC, he declared that he has spoken with Colonel Schwarzkopf and that the governor was "satisfied that the police have done nothing anywhere nearly approaching the so-called third degree…I stand squarely behind Colonel Schwarzkopf"

Violet's funeral services were held on June 15th at the Green Leaf Chapel and she was buried near her former employer, the late Senator Dwight Morrow in Brookside Cemetery, Englewood. One of the most tragic figures in the Lindbergh kidnapping saga, her story is recounted and debated in nearly every publication concerning the case. There are extensive files about her investigation and even some of her personal possessions are in the collections of the New Jersey State Police Museum in West Trenton.

While much is written about the movements of Violet Sharp around March 1, 1932 very little, if anything, has been printed regarding Violet's life prior to moving to Englewood. Little is known about her family save for her sister Emily[39] who does appear along with her in the literature.

The Sharp family was from Bradfield, Berkshire in southeast England. Violet's father, George Sharp, was from Bradfield where he was born in 1874. Her mother Lucy Smith, was a year younger than George, and hailed from Hampstead Norreys where she and George were married on September 17, 1898. George, like his father, was a brick maker and his father-in-law, Job Smith, was a bricklayer.

George and Lucy had six children. The eldest, Bessie, was born in 1899. She married Arthur J. Burbage in Bradford, Wiltshire, in the spring of 1925 and eventually moved to Salisbury. In the spring of 1932, Arthur suffered a massive stroke. He was only 31 years old at the time. Her mother wrote that Bessie was "very upset as Arthur was brought home & he is so helpless just like a baby so it's jolly rough luck on them as they are both young…"

Charley Sharp was born in 1901. He enlisted in the army and was discharged sometime around 1927. He and his wife Vivian then lived with his parents while he worked in his father's business.

Mary Sharp was born in 1906 and married Leslie J. Garnsey, a butler, in 1930 in Hagley, Worcestershire. They later moved to nearby Stourbridge. James, the youngest of the Sharp boys, was born in 1907. He, too, enlisted in the army – the 1st Battalion Royal Berkshire Regiment. He was last stationed in Dinapore, West Bengal, India. He had enlisted around 1925 and was very eager to return to England when he was discharged in 1932 or 1933. When he returned home he was unemployed and lived with his older sister in Birmingham.

The youngest child of George and Lucy was their daughter Emily. Born in 1909 she was very close with her sister Violet. They traveled together to Canada and the United States where they took jobs as domestic servants.

Violet Sharp was the third child and was born on July 25, 1904 in the little Berskhire village of Tutts Clump about eight miles from Reading. Shortly after she was born, the family had moved to 1 Rose Cottage in Beenham in West Berkshire east of Newbury. They attended St. Mary's Church and the children attended the Beenham School. Both Violet and Emily left school at age 14 – Violet in 1918 and her sister in 1923.

Since 1919, Violet held several domestic service jobs in England obtained through Nelly Webb's Domestic Agency in London. One such position was working for Lady Hester Chetwode, the wife of Field Marshal Philip Walhouse Chetwode, 1st Baron Chetwode. He was a British cavalry officer who later became Commander-in-Chief in India and his photograph was found among Violet's personal possessions after her death. Violet   had been working for Mrs. Donaldson-Hudson of Cheswardine Hall in Market Drayton, Shropshire for over two years when, in 1929 she and her sister Emily decided it was time for a little adventure. On August 10th they set sail from Southampton for Quebec, Canada and it was at this time that Emily changed her name to Edna.

They stayed in Canada until December 1930 when they to Englewood, New Jersey. Emily went to work for Elizabeth Chilton, a close friend of the Morrow family. On May 13th, the Richard T. Hutchinson Bureau for Domestic Help on Madison Avenue in New York placed Violet with Elizabeth Morrow at $85 a month. She worked as Mrs. Morrow's waitress and was given a room on the third floor of the mansion.

Emily had only worked for Miss Chilton for five or six months before she found herself in the hospital. It is not known what the reason was, but she spent three months in the hospital and then two weeks in a convalescent home in White Plains, New York. When she was released, she went to work for a Mrs. Reiker in Port Chester, New York and, after only five months went to work for Mrs. McDowell in New York City.

Emily would see her sister at least once a week. They would go to the movies, shop, go on dates and probably occasionally visit a speakeasy. They were two young women thousands of miles away from home out to enjoy life's adventures in the Big Apple.

In 1931 their kid brother, James, was gearing up for his eventual discharge from the British Army. He could not wait to get out of the military and start making money. On September 10th, he wrote to Violet from India saying that "I have been trying to get to New Jersey from here, but I don't know if I shall go or not yet…is there much work out there for men as I don't think I shall stay in England. There don't seem any work there and all I am after is money."

Jim wanted Violet and Emily to return to England so they could "start some thing on our own when we get in England. I shall have about £100 when I get home – that is if I could thin[k] of a nice money making job. Dad is too slow, all he thinks about is drink, that would be no good to us." He knew of Violet's plans to return to England in the spring, around the same time as Emily. "Vi you say you get home some time in the spring, what did you think of doing, staying the summer in England, I would just love to be out there with you…Vi I hope we all three gets in England together we will have a royal time for a bit what say you?"

Violet, Emily and Jim seemed like your typical young siblings who were always having a good time together. Jim found adventure in India and his sisters in the United States. But these adventures apart were supposed to be short lived, with everyone reuniting in England. But the events of March 1, 1932 put a crimp in their plans. Violet would not be coming home.

Of the three, Violet was the most emotional to the point of being unstable. This was most apparent during her questioning by the police. However, there were earlier signs of it back in England.

According to Emily, Violet told her on a couple of occasions that she had been married years before in London, when she was just 17 years old. She said his name was George Payne. When asked about this after Violet's suicide he denied it and there was no record of the marriage ever found. Emily said it had only been mentioned "in passing" and their mother, Lucy, first told her of it before they left for Canada. Violet allegedly kept the marriage secret from their mother, "…until he was supposed to be dead. My mother said, 'I don't believe it' to which Violet retorted, "Fine, it didn't happen then!'"

The alleged marriage came to light in 1929 when Violet applied for her passport. Her application was delayed because she needed to have letters of recommendation from her previous employers and some of them were addressed to Violet Payne; she had applied for her passport as Violet Payne. The matter was eventually resolved and she was issued her passport.

After her suicide, Scotland Yard was asked to investigate the alleged marriage, but they found no record of it at Somerset House in London. They did learn that although Violet said that he had died, George Payne was very much alive and living in London. They paid him a visit at his home at 7 Aubrey Mansions on Lisson Street in the Marylebone section of the city.

The investigators learned that George Payne was born in 1869, making him 35 years older than Violet. He married Ellen Cone in 1896 and they had one daughter, Winifred Annie who was born shortly thereafter. She later married a Mr. Little and they were living with her parents on Lisson Street.

George Payne was a printer's stock keeper and in early 1927 he met Violet when they both worked for Mr. Pearce-Leigh in Gloucester Square, Paddington. Payne was employed as a butler and Violet as a parlor maid. They worked there for six months, until the Pearce-Leighs moved to a country home.

George stated that he and Violet were never intimate; at most they went to the movies together. After leaving the Pearce-Leighs employ they never worked together again. Violet would write him and they would meet for walks whenever she got back to London. George set up an address for the letters – 37 St. Martins Court – because he did not want them going to his home.

George remained married to Ellen for the rest of his life. He died at home on June 15, 1942 from liver cancer and is buried in Hanwell Cemetery,

Uxbridge Road in London. He was 72 years old when he died. Violet would have been only 38.

Violet came across in her questioning by the police as being very excitable and highly emotional, on the verge of a breakdown at times. Could the intense police interrogations have been amplified in her mind to make them more than they actually were? Was her close friendship with George Payne just that, a friendship but one magnified and distorted by Violet to the point that she actually believed that they had been married? Why would she tell some of her employers that she was Mrs. Payne instead of Miss Sharp? It appears that Violet's excitability and her penchant for fantasy and blowing things out of proportion was not unique to her dealings with the State Police.

Rather than a physician keeping an eye on her during her interrogations she really needed the services of a psychiatrist, someone who could see the warning signs and give her the help she needed. The last letter she wrote was to her best friend Fan Simmons in Wales. It was clearly written by someone on the verge of a nervous breakdown, feeling the pressure of the police interrogations, the sadness of murder of the Lindbergh baby, and reports of illness from home. Everything around her was falling apart:

> We have all been questioned by the police and I have been in hospital a week with a poisoned throat – had my tonsils out – and I only weigh 7 stones the least I have ever been in my life and I just feel as weak as a rat. I want to come home so much but I cannot because the country…they would think I knew something about the baby. You have no idea what we have been through. When the police had me for questioning I fainted [twice] in 2 hours…Life is getting so sad, I really don't think there is anything to live for any more…I had a letter from home to say my sister's husband has had a stroke and he is just helpless as a baby can't move or do anything. He is only 31. My mother is not so good and Edna could not get a job out here so she has gone home. The heat is terrible it takes all the pep out of you. You can't go out, it is too hot and we are not going to North Haven…I have been here only 2 years now, quite an old servant, don't you think? [40]

Violet Sharp is one of the most tragic figures in the whole Lindbergh Kidnapping saga. She died feeling alone and helpless, trapped by the events swirling around her facing the accusatory stares of everyone she passed. She was 27 years old when she died. Violet is buried in an unmarked grave in a foreign land thousands of miles from home.

13. Colonel H. Norman Schwarzkopf in 1935

14. Trooper Hugo Stockburger

15. Top Left to Right: John J. Lamb; Arthur T. Keaten; Samuel Leon; William Horn; John Wallace & Nuncio "Nick" DeGaetano

**16. Top Left to Right: Eugene Haussling, Andrew
Zapolsky and Lewis Bornmann**

17. William Allen and his wife Helen Jennings Allen

18. Violet Sharp (sitting) and her sister
Emily (Edna)

19. Violet's best friend, Fan Simmons

20. Violet Sharp's Funeral in Englewood, NJ (June 19, 1932)

21. Associate Justice Thomas Trenchard

22. The Flemington Jury

23. Clockwise from top left: C. Lloyd Fisher, Egbert Rosecrans with Hauptmann, Egbert Rosecrans, Frederick Pope

24. Anthony Hauck, Jr.

20. Associate Justice Thomas Trenchard

When Bruno Richard Hauptmann was arrested and extradited to New Jersey for trial, he entered a complex judicial system that had evolved from the English and Colonial system of the 18th Century. In 1935, New Jersey's Supreme Court was not the ultimate appellate court as it is today; the Court of Errors and Appeals held that position. The Supreme Court, with its Chief Justice and eight associate justices was, however, the ultimate court with jurisdiction over civil and criminal cases.

The justices of the Supreme Court were each assigned one of nine judicial districts, or circuits. These districts encompassed the twenty-one counties of the state and the justice presided over the circuit courts in each county that fell into his district. These included the Orphans' Court, which had jurisdiction over guardians and executorships, the Court of Quarter Session, which was responsible for general criminal cases except for murder and treason, and the higher criminal court known as the Court of Oyer and Terminer.[41] This last court had jurisdiction over all criminal cases and "except in counties having a population of 300,000 or more, a justice of the Supreme Court must preside over it, and the [county] judge of the Court of Common Plea may or may not sit with him."

At the time, it was speculated in the press that Hunterdon County Common Plea Judge Adam O. Robbins would sit with Trenchard to assist during the Hauptmann trial; however, as it was the prerogative of the Supreme Court Justice to sit alone, that is just what he did. Robbins' sole task was to preside over the selection of the 150-member jury pool in November 1934.[42]

Hunterdon County's Court of Oyer and Terminer fell under the cognizance of Associate Justice Thomas W. Trenchard. Trenchard was a venerable elder jurist who had been on the bench since 1899. He was a "tall, dignified, scholarly looking man with a keen mind and a forceful demeanor." Noted for his decisiveness, he was a "stickler for the proprieties" in the courtroom.

Thomas Whitaker Trenchard was the son of William B. and Anna M. Goulder Trenchard of South Jersey. He was born on December 13, 1863 in Centerton, Salem County, New Jersey. Shortly after his birth the family moved to neighboring Cumberland County where his father served as County Clerk for many years.

Thomas Trenchard attended public school in Burlington. In 1882 he graduated from the South Jersey Institute, a boarding school for boys and girls. He then attended law school while working in the Bridgeton law office of Potter & Nixon.

After graduation, Trenchard was admitted to the State Bar as an attorney in 1886 and then in 1893 as a counselor. He continued to practice law in Bridgeton and served as the Solicitor for the Bridgeton Board of Health until 1899. At this time the Governor of New Jersey, Foster Voorhees, appointed him as Judge in Cumberland County's Common Pleas court, a position he held until 1906.

Because of his distinguished judicial career, many people do not realize that Thomas Trenchard was also active politically in the state. For example, in 1888 he was elected to the State Assembly for one term and in 1896 he was appointed as a Presidential Elector, casting ballots for President McKinley in the Electoral College.

His most important appointment, however, came on June 8, 1906 when Governor Edward Stokes appointed Trenchard as an Associate Justice of the Supreme Court of New Jersey. He was filling a vacancy left by the death of Justice Jonathan Dixon and the following year he was re-appointed to a full term. Trenchard would be re-appointed five more times in his career.

When Trenchard received his full appointment to the Supreme Court he and his wife, the former Harriet Manning of Red Bank, moved from Bridgeton to Trenton. They resided at 816 Riverside Avenue in a house overlooking the Delaware River for the rest of their lives.

For many years, Justice Trenchard presided over the First Judicial Circuit that included both Camden and Atlantic Counties. He was regarded as "a jurist of the highest character. He had been tireless in denouncing the scandalous misconduct of the Atlantic [County] officials, and charged grand jury after grand jury to bring the guilty men to the bar of justice." Then, when Associate Justice Ludlow died in 1911, it opened a vacancy in the Third Circuit, which encompassed Mercer, Hunterdon and Warren Counties. Trenchard switched to this circuit, where he remained for the rest of his career.

As demonstrated by his judicial and political service, Trenchard was a very civic-minded individual. He organized and served as president of the Cumberland County Bar Association and was active with the Sons of the American Revolution. He also served on the Board of Managers of the Home for Disabled Soldiers, Sailors, Marines and their Wives in Vineland, New Jersey. All of this was overshadowed, however, by the 32 days he spent presiding over the trial of Bruno Richard Hauptmann.

While it is not within the scope of this book to debate the fairness of the Hauptmann Trial, certain aspects should be highlighted[43]. Trenchard was known to be "a very considerate and courteous man who…at times seemed almost obsessed with the comfort and health of his lawyers and jurors, assuming the role of a benevolent patriarch." He also tended to "bend over backwards for defense lawyers" in criminal cases. Ludovic Kennedy admits in his book, *The Airman and The Carpenter,* that Trenchard was fair, especially in his explanations of the law. However, after Trenchard charged the jury and sent them into chambers to ponder Hauptmann's guilt or innocence, defense attorney Frederick Pope moved for a mistrial "on the grounds that Judge Trenchard's charge to the jury was heavily opinionated and patently biased in favor of the State." Ironically, it was Charles Lindbergh who was one of the first to observe that "Trenchard's charge read more impartially than it sounded. 'For instance', he later told Harold Nicolson[44], 'he kept on saying to the jury, in going over some of Hauptmann's evidence, "Do you believe that?" Now that sounds all right in print. But what he actually said was, "Do *you* believe *that?*"'"

Another problem at the trial was the overcrowding of the courtroom with "crowds of spectators standing and impinging on the aisles and passageways." Trenchard was aware of the problem but "he received indifferent co-operation from the court officers, frequently admonish[ing] them to keep order instead of 'sitting around in the courtroom having no oversight over the audience.'"

> Some of the officers are here in charge of the jury. Many of them are at the doors, I assume, but there are officers sitting around, apparently in this courtroom, having no oversight at all over the audience. The officers are here primarily for the purpose of keeping order…the court has to rely upon the officers who are here for that purpose and I want these officers hereafter to take their stations down in the main body of the court room where this confusion and laughter

arises about every fifteen minutes. I want these officers to see to it that that confusion and laughter is stopped.

Almost on a daily basis, he had to admonish the public attending the trial for disrupting the proceedings with laughter and applause. As early as January 4th, the third day of the trial, there was disruptive laughter and Trenchard had to interrupt the proceedings to say the following:

> This confusion and laughter is getting to be a kind of nuisance. Unless it is stopped, I shall have to have the courtroom cleared. If people want to remain here and give the court a reasonable opportunity to reasonably try this case, they will have to keep quiet. Otherwise, we will have to get along without any spectators.

Admonitions and threats to clear the courtroom continued for almost the entire duration of the trial with little effect. Trenchard did what he could to maintain order. Oscar Hallam, chairman of the committee appointed to consider the fairness of the Hauptmann Trial, concluded, "The court's orders were adequate, but their enforcement in the little courtroom was committed to temporary bailiffs who did not measure up to the job."

Even the attorneys added to the problem of overcrowding. According to a January 26, 1935 article in the *New York Times*, Justice Trenchard called both the defense and prosecution attorneys together to discuss their practice "…of issuing subpoenas ostensibly to 'witnesses' who [would] be called upon to testify, but in reality [were] to friends seeking a seat in the courtroom. Sheriff Curtiss said that more than 100 such subpoenas were issued" for one session.

While the attorneys pandered to the press and the rich and famous pushed and shoved their way into the courtroom, Trenchard continued on, as he always had, on an even keel. During the trial, he received a letter from James Hardyman of Middlesex, England. In the letter Hardyman quotes the January 11th issue of the *Daily Telegraph:*

> Judge Trenchard…arrives at the courthouse…at 9:30 each morning, driven by a colored chauffeur. Wearing a heavy fleeced coat, with a fur collar that almost hides his tall, ample frame, and a grey tweed hat of the deerstalker type, he has an almost boyish appearance, despite his 73 years. He carries a small package gingerly under his arm – his lunch which has been carefully prepared by his wife. He blinks as

the cameras explode around him, but never gets angry with 'the boys,' as he calls them.

The trial continued for 32 days and its historic verdict of guilty with no mercy was rendered on February 13, 1935. Although Hauptmann appealed, going as far as to request a hearing before the United States Supreme Court (which was denied), the verdict stood. After thirty-five years on the Supreme Court, Trenchard never had one of his murder cases reversed.

Thomas Trenchard continued to try cases in the Supreme Court until his retirement on January 24, 1941. He was succeeded by Justice Frederic R. Colie.

Three years earlier on February 9, 1938, Harriet Manning Trenchard, his wife of 47 years, had died. Just over a year after his retirement, at age 79, Justice Trenchard suffered a cerebral hemorrhage and died a few days later on July 23, 1942 in Trenton. Reverend Don Clyde Kyte of the Second (Central) Baptist Church in Trenton conducted his funeral.[45] The honorary pallbearers were the sixteen members of the Court of Errors and Appeals of which Trenchard was a member. He was buried next to his wife in the Old Broad Street Presbyterian Church Cemetery in Bridgeton, New Jersey.

21. The Flemington Talesmen

The sixth amendment to the Constitution of the United States guarantees the right of the accused to an impartial jury of the jurisdiction where the alleged crime was committed. Because the kidnapping and murder of Charles Lindbergh Jr., occurred at the Lindbergh Estate in East Amwell, New Jersey, the jury convened for the trial of Bruno Richard Hauptmann was comprised of citizens from throughout rural Hunterdon County. Jury Commissioner Charles Holcombe and Hunterdon County Sheriff John Curtiss drew a pool of 150 potential petit jurors in November 1934. On the first two days of the trial in January 1935 the final twelve talesmen, or jurors, were selected.

While there is an abundance of information about the trial itself, detailed information about the lives of the jurors is scarce. They truly were twelve ordinary citizens from the heart of rural New Jersey.

Four women and eight men were selected to serve on Hauptmann's petit jury. The jury was sequestered across the street from the courthouse in nine rooms on the third floor of the Union Hotel. It was here that they lived in near isolation for 43 days and 42 nights guarded by four deputy sheriffs. They had no contact with the outside world, having been admonished by Justice Trenchard to "…be very careful not to discuss the case with anyone, not to read the newspapers, not to listen at the radio and not to attend public gatherings."

Their meals were served in the Hotel's dining room, but "because the hotel dining room crowd stared, screens covered with flower-prigged wallpaper were set up to shield the jurors." The jurors passed their time inside by playing cards – usually bridge, listening to phonograph records and reading censored newspapers. On the weekends they were treated to bus rides into the countryside. Judge Trenchard ordered them to "take plenty of exercise in the open air" so, looking like waddling ducks lined up in a row, they would take daily walks through town under the strict supervision of the constables who shielded them from contact with the public.

They were in their own little world and they quickly realized that they had to create their own civilization to go with it. "One of the ladies was nominated to do the beauty shop for the other women of the jury…[and] among the men a haircutter was developed…Laundry had to be done, particularly those mysterious clothes women wear. One of the women volunteered as a laundress. The washbasin served as the tub…we rigged up a sort of gymnasium…out in the narrow hall…Tug-of-war was one god game…and the women usually won. We found that the side where there was the most weight generally came out ahead."

So who were the ladies and gentlemen who comprised what one newspaper referred to as *the gallery of life and death*?

Fifty-year-old Charles Walton, Sr., a machinist from High Bridge, New Jersey, was the first chosen and was thereby appointed the Jury Foreman. Born on January 3, 1884 in Pennsylvania, he was the eldest of ten children. He moved to Hunterdon County and was employed by the Taylor Wharton Iron and Steel Company of High Bridge for twenty-five years.[46] Walton had been earning $6 a day however, during the Hauptmann Trial, the court only paid him $3.

Charles loved baseball and in his younger days he pitched on a semi-professional team. The press actually stole a photograph of him in his High Bridge Athletic Association baseball uniform from his family home and they used it to illustrate news stories throughout the trial!

Charles Walton was married to Edith Thompson and they had four children: three sons and a daughter. Following in his father's footsteps, their oldest son, Charles Jr., also worked as a machinist at Taylor Wharton. Their second son, Thompson, was a student at the Springfield, Massachusetts Y. M. C. A. College. Unfortunately nothing is known of their younger son James.

Marie, their youngest child and only daughter, was just nine years old at the time of the trial. Not quite three decades later, in 1962, her parents would move in with her. Three years later, her mother passed away.

Charles Walton, Sr. lived a full life. His remaining years were spent living with his daughter and keeping active with the Hobart Masonic Lodge in High Bridge. He was 97 years old when he passed away in Hunterdon Medical Center on December 23, 1981. "Serious B. B. Charlie", his nickname during the trial, was buried in Evergreen Cemetery in Clinton, New Jersey.

Juror number two was Rosie Pill, the 200-pound widowed housekeeper from Califon, New Jersey. After her husband Frank, a clothing merchant, died she rented a room from her son Joseph, his wife Marie and their three children. Rosie's other son, Frank, lived at Hempstead, Long Island, where he taught high school.

Her son Joseph was a local businessman and his wife a public school teacher. While they were at work, Rosie would care for her grandchildren, J. Donald, Kenneth and Wallace. Rosie would also pass the time doing beadwork and her neighbors all declared to the press, "she is one of the nicest women we ever met!"

That may be, but she was noted by the State Police detectives who investigated the potential jurors as only a "fair type juror" because her reputation was "questionable [as she is a] gossiper." Regardless, both the defense and prosecution wanted her and "Good Girl Rosie" was selected for the Hauptmann Jury.

After the trial, she returned home to continue caring for her grandchildren. Rosie was only 65 years old when, on January 21, 1941, she died at the Glen Memorial Hospital.

Verna Cole Snyder was Juror number three. The press, who was obsessed with the weight of both Rosie Pill and Verna Snyder, declared that her "...261 pounds made her a weighty problem." On January 26th humiliating headlines informed readers that of the two jurors that were ill, the "261-lb woman ate too much." Apparently she had been suffering from a cold since the start of the trial and, as the State doctor R. S. Fuhrman declared, overeating only exasperated the symptoms. The press, apparently not having enough news from the Trial of the Century to fill their pages, reported that Verna "ate steak with a pile of mashed potatoes and noodles, two pieces of pie, three cups of coffee and fifteen rolls. Later she danced with other jurors to the strains of *Casey Jones* on a phonograph. This morning she breakfasted in bed and complained of feeling unwell."

Even Walter Winchell was quick to add his own brand of insult. His January 30, 1935 article ran the headline: "Smasho! Flash! Crash!!!" His pejorative article continued, "Verna Snyder, Juror No. 3, who tips the Toledos at 261, is said to have fallen out of bed in her Union Hotel boudoir night before last. First rumors were that there had been an earthquake."

In addition to their weight obsession, the press was fixated on Verna's coat. She was rarely, if ever, seen without it. And this, too, made headlines: "Three Women Jurors Remove Hats; Fourth Sits Bundled in Coat." Any photograph showing the jury almost always made reference to Snyder's ever-present frock.

There was more to Verna Snyder than her weight and apparel but because that seemed to be all that the press reported details about her life are scant. Nicknamed "Contented Verna" by her fellow jurors, she was born on December 17, 1897 in Hunterdon County and she was a member of the Centerville Methodist Church. She married Fred Snyder, the village blacksmith, around 1930. They had one adopted son, seven-year-old Jack.

Fred was devoted to Verna and "each day [he] came to Flemington and stood on the sidewalk in front of the Union Hotel to watch [his wife] carry her 261 pounds on a slow, majestic walk on the veranda. He waves diffidently and then turns slowly toward home."

Her husband passed away in 1943, but Verna survived him by thirty-one years. She died on December 15, 1974 just two days shy of her 77th birthday. It is not known what ever happened to her coat.

Juror number 4, Charles F. Snyder – no relation to Verna – was born on January 9, 1890. He was considered a "prosperous farmer" from Clinton, New Jersey, where he was the secretary of the Annandale Dairy Association.

Charles had courtroom experience having served on three previous murder juries, including the Conde murder trial in 1921 "for which a second degree verdict was returned."

"Dimples", as the Hauptmann jurors knew him, was married with two sons, seventeen-year-old Harry and nine-year-old Frank. The time Charles spent sequestered on the Hauptmann jury put a great strain on his family. The farm animals did not care that he was called away to perform his civic duty in Flemington, so it fell to his son Harry, who had to skip school, to help his grandfather run the farm in his father's absence. Eventually, Charles returned to the farm and life continued as before until his death in December 1967.

Ethel Morgan Stockton continues to be one of the most popular and well known of the jurors. Referred to in the press as the "beauty in the box", she almost always wore red and was considered the most attractive woman on the jury.

She was married to Elmer Stockton[47], a machinist at the Milford Paper Mill in Milford, New Jersey and they lived with their seven-year-old son Robert in Pattenburg where she sang in a choir.

Ethel's husband and brother-in-law were both in the large jury pool that was assembled in November 1934 but neither one was chosen for the final panel. In fact, the State Police reported on December 30, 1934 that they had learned that her brother-in-law was "a rattle brain and no good for either side."

Ethel on the other hand was far from being a "rattle brain." After graduating high school, she took a stenographic course at Churchmen's Business School in Easton, Pennsylvania. She became acquainted with criminal law when she worked as a stenographer for James V. Aller, the Hunterdon County Prosecutor from 1927 to 1932. "During Aller's five-year term, [she] worked at his elbow. 'I think she drew most of the indictments for me while I was in office – under my dictation.'" At the time of Hauptmann's trial she was working two-and-a-half days a week for a former state attorney's law office in Clinton. She continued to work in law offices for the rest of her career.

Because Ethel was sequestered during the trial and her husband worked nights, her son Robert – and his black and white bird dog 'King' – stayed with his grandfather. Her son was upset because he believed that his mother was actually in jail. He was only convinced otherwise when he was taken to the courthouse so he could actually see her sitting in the jury box.

One day, Ethel inadvertently caused a stir at the trial when she innocently smiled at Hauptmann as he took the witness stand to testify. He noticed the smile and was convinced that she did not think he was a "bad guy." The ever-diligent press also noticed the smile and "Juror Smiles At Hauptmann" headlines ran in all the papers the following day.

Ethel was born on January 19, 1902 and her birthday fell right in the middle of the trial. Her fellow jurors, who dubbed her "Chubby-Spitfire Stockton", threw a party for her where they served angel food cake and sang. It was a very welcome break from their routine and they "did their best to make the occasion a gala affair."

For several years after the trial ended, Ethel received many requests to speak at various functions throughout New Jersey and the surrounding areas. One invitation she accepted was from The Bar Association of Nassau County, New York. They invited her to speak at their monthly meeting on February 25, 1937 as one of their guest speakers. The invitation included meals, a hotel room and train fare for both her and her husband.

Invitations such as these were not the only requests Ethel Stockton received. On February 13, 1935 – the day the verdict was rendered – Cirilo Nelic of Buenos Ares, Argentina, wrote the following to her: "I saw your photo in the *Diario Critico*, fell in love with you and want you to marry me." The plan was for her to come to Argentina to marry him and then, together, they would return to the United States where he would become a citizen. A little flattered and greatly amused, Ethel kept this letter (and the envelope) in her scrapbook.

In 1980 Ethel retired from attorney Albert Rylak's office in Clinton. She moved to Ocala, Florida where she spent the rest of her life in retirement. She died on February 28, 2002, just one day before the 70th anniversary of the kidnapping. She was 100 years old.

Well-dressed forty-two-year-old Elmer Smith was "an answer to a maiden's prayer." Or so thought the Hauptmann Jury. A former justice of the peace from Lambertville, New Jersey he retired as an insurance salesman in 1933 and moved to California with his wife and son for one year. No sooner did they return to New Jersey Elmer was chosen as the fifth member of the Hauptmann jury. Elmer Smith lived in the Trenton area until his death in April 1986 at age 94.

The youngest juror was Robert Cravatt, a 28-year-old single schoolteacher from High Bridge, New Jersey. He was an assistant educational director of a Civilian Conservation Camp (CCC) at Voorhees, Somerset County and the treasurer of the High Bridge Basketball Team. His father, Archibald, worked for many years at the Taylor Wharton Iron and Steel Works along side Charles Walton, the jury foreman.

"Pretty Boy Bob" was well liked by his fellow jurors. He guarded his privacy diligently and so very little is known of the rest of his life other than that he moved from New Jersey to Bull Shoals, Arkansas.

Annandale resident Philip Hockenbury was the eighth juror selected. He had been a track inspector for the Central Rail Road of New Jersey since 1920. When he was called to jury duty in Flemington, he reluctantly left his wife and three children behind. Reporters, wanting to learn every tidbit about the jury as possible, frequently tried to interview their family members. However, Mrs. Hockenbury refused to speak to the press during the trial: "A caller at the Hockenbury door in Annandale was in the process of explaining his identity to the buxom lady who opened it a few inches when she interrupted him most abruptly. 'Nothin' doin'!' she exclaimed and the door swung shut with a considerable impact."

"Jafsie", as he was affectionately known, died tragically on May 8, 1936 when he was struck by a freight train near the High Bridge train station. He was repairing a switch when he was struck by the westbound train and was killed instantly. He was only 56 years old.

George Voorhees, juror number nine, was, like Charles Snyder, considered a prosperous farmer. Hailing from Bissel, New Jersey, he was married with two grown children. He and his wife raised horses that he used to race in countryside meets.

Voorhees was a very prominent citizen who took an active part in local and civic affairs and was nicknamed "Horsie" by his fellow jurors.

The fourth woman on the Hauptmann Jury was May F. Brelsford. She was the only native of Flemington to serve on the jury. Her husband was an electrician and they lived on Broad Street where she cared for her two stepchildren, Jack and Mary.

May was very active in the Episcopal Church and was a past matron of the Darcy Chapter of the Order of the Eastern Star. "Giggles" was thought to be a "fair type juror" who was a "proper American and not easily led."

Liscom C. Case, juror number eleven, was the juror who almost caused the Hauptmann Trial to be declared a mistrial. He was around 60 years old and was in very poor health. He suffered with heart trouble for many years, which is why he retired in 1925 as foreman of carpenters of the Leigh Valley Railroad. During the trial he suffered a slight heart attack. "He complained of the walk up two flights of stairs to the jurors' rooms in the Union Hotel." Since there was no alternate juror to replace him, "the death or complete physical collapse of Case would result in a mistrial and the entire evidence would have to be presented again." Dr. R. S. Fuhrman, the State's doctor, reported that Case's condition "was not serious and danger of collapse during the trial was remote...the frequent climbing of two flights of stairs in the jury's hotel and in the court house each day had put an added tax on Case's heart." Therefore, Case was ordered to remain in his room and his meals were brought to him and he was served lunch in the judge's chambers in the courthouse. Of course, the press jumped on this, declaring, "Extraordinary precautions were taken...to prevent a heart attack incapacitating Juror No. 11, Liscum C. Case. Dr. Fuhrman...prescribed a regimen intended to safeguard the juror's health."

"Silent Cal" survived the trial and returned to his carpentry shop "out behind his house in a white-washed little woodshed, snug in the hills of Hunterdon County." He lived alone, his wife had died in 1928 and they had no children. Liscum's heart condition finally caught up with him and he died at home on December 29, 1935. His funeral was held on January 2, 1936 – exactly one year after the Hauptmann Case went to trial. Reverend R. D. Driscoll of the Grandin Presbyterian Church officiated and he was buried in Grandin Cemetery, in the heart of Hunterdon County less than one mile from the town of Franklin where he was born.

The last jury member chosen, Howard V. Biggs, was an unemployed accountant and former assessor in Hunterdon County. He lived in Annandale with his wife and two sons, Howard Jr. and Kenneth. They were married on February 13, 1908 and he had never been away from his wife before. His wife was miserable because of her husband's sequestering. A trained nurse, she was unable to go to work because of his absence from home. She bemoaned to the press, "I feel it more because he was the sort of man who stayed home nights and never goes out anywhere without me."

Unfortunately, "Chatter Box Biggs" is one of those anonymous members of the Flemington jury about whom little else is known. Anonymous or not, his family shared the same difficulties as most of the other jury members' families who missed their husbands and wives and mothers and fathers terribly. "In a survey of jurors' homes, *Evening Journal* reporters found wives, husbands and children lonesome and impatient for the return of their kin… some are beginning to feel the financial sacrifice by the jury service."

Three dollars a day was all they were earned for serving on the jury, a total of $129 for the entire trial. This could be why many of the jurors showed interest in a "lucrative theatrical show offer for a twelve-week tour of the country." Each juror was offered $300 a week ($500 for Charles Walton, the Jury Foreman) and a luxury tour of the country in return for the "re-enactment of the semi-hysterical scenes in the jury room, where Verna Snyder…broke down and wept as she cast her ballot for death; and Robert Cravatt…held out for mercy until the fifth and last ballot." William Donoghue of the *New York Evening Star* wrote "Mrs. Verna Snyder, the 291 pound housewife of Centerville, will go along…If the proposed contract is accepted, some of the jurors will be leaving the confines of Hunterdon County for the first time in their lives. As [her husband] Snyder said, 'It will help broaden Verna.'" Money and travel aside, the jurors realized that the show was in very bad taste and the deal fell through.

At least while they were in the jury box and deliberating in the jury room for those long eleven and a half hours, each juror took their job very seriously. They were, however, human and at times they appeared to be bored. During Hauptmann's testimony Rosie Pill actually fell asleep! "Mrs. Verna Snyder, the enigma of the jury…looked bored. Her eyes roved and sometimes she impatiently tapped her foot." Another newspaper noted "the chins of the male jurors in the rear row rested on their chests. There were many sighs, many deep yawns, among the prisoner's peers."

Yet, when the experts testified, they were attentive. Liscom Case, the sickly carpenter, was at his best when Arthur Koehler, the wood expert, testified. He was seen to straighten up and lean over the jury rail in order to get a closer look at the exhibits Koehler happened to be describing.

They took their deliberations very seriously. They were afraid of hidden microphones that may have been planted in the jury room. "The first thing they did before they began their deliberation was to search behind drapes and under chairs. The table was removed to the center of the room and the jurors kept voices low…to prevent eavesdropping. "…The jury, which had deliberated for more than eleven hours, went at the task in the most painstaking fashion. [They] examined the exhibits closely [and] sent out for a magnifying glass with which they studied the handwriting…Led by Liscom Case, the carpenter, they studied the plane markings on the ladder."

They did not want to rush to judgment. After they decided that Hauptmann was indeed guilty there were five additional ballots to determine his sentence. The first one was taken to see where the jury stood so there was no prior discussion. It resulted in seven voting for the electric chair and five for life. Rosie Pill, Verna Snyder, Elmer Smith, Philip Hockenbury and Robert Cravatt were the holdouts. After some discussion, a second vote was taken and both Rosie and Verna decided to vote for death. Hockenbury was finally convinced to switch his vote on the third ballot and on the fourth Elmer Smith finally agreed to an execution. Cravatt was the only one that needed still refused to condemn Hauptmann to the electric chair.

Deliberations continued and on the fifth and final ballot the vote was unanimous. According to Charles Walton, "the lone hold-out…wanted to vote for conviction but was afraid of reprisals. The reluctant juror had to be convinced and the jury spent the remainder of the time deciding on a second or first degree murder conviction."

During the ensuing years since their deliberations, new interpretations and insight regarding the evidence and witnesses at the trial have come to light. Access to investigation reports that were once kept separate from rival departments and confidential from the public can now be reviewed and critiqued and investigative and forensic techniques have progressed in leaps and bounds. One can only wonder how this new knowledge would have affected the jury in 1935 – had they had access to it. Ethel Stockton said in a 1982 interview with reporter Ed Mack that FBI records, State Police Files and other new findings have created doubts in her mind about the State's case against Hauptmann:

> I'm certainly not ready to say that any of this could have
> changed the verdict, but there are questions raised today that
> the defense didn't mention at all.

Hauptmann's lead attorney, Edward J. Reilly, treated the Flemington Talesmen with contempt. The press filled many inches of column space with insulting descriptions and belittling remarks about them. The world was made to think of these twelve men and women as simple country hicks. Jury Foreman Charles Walton phrased it best when he said this about his fellow jurors: "We ranged from farmers through the trades and office workers to a justice of the peace. Not one of us was great, but no dunces were in the box. None of us had had such a stuffing of education that we had lost our common sense."

22. The Experts

The Lindbergh Kidnapping Case is considered to be one of the first cases to be prosecuted based predominantly on forensic evidence. Leading experts in handwriting analysis, wood examination, psychological profiling and fingerprint identification testified at the Hauptmann Trial in 1935.

Forensics was still a new concept in American law enforcement in the 1930s. The concept of "chain of custody" for items held as evidence and the scientific handling of crime scenes were just coming into being. The New Jersey State Police did not even have their own scientific laboratory yet and had to rely on the Squibb Pharmaceutical Company for analysis of evidence and the remains of the baby found in the woods by William Allen.

The idea of fingerprinting for criminal investigations began in Europe in the 19th Century. By 1900 the science of fingerprinting being practiced in Great Britain but was still relatively new in the United States at the time of the Lindbergh baby kidnapping in 1932. The State Police sent their fingerprint expert, Trooper Frank Kelly, to the crime scene on the night of March 1st to dust for fingerprints. He found none in the baby's nursery, except for a few on the crib that belonged to the Lindbergh child and he was unable to find any on the kidnap ladder.

The New York City Police Department suggested that Dr. Erastus Hudson should be called to see what he could find.

Born in 1888 in Plattsburg, New York, Erastus Mead Hudson was a 1913 Harvard Graduate. He then entered the College of Physicians and Surgeons in New York, graduating in 1917 as a specialist in body chemistry and bacteriology. Upon graduation he enlisted in the Navy Medical Corps as a Lieutenant Junior Grade and served as a medical officer aboard the U. S. S. Leviathan.

During the First World War, he was stationed in England and it was there that he became interested in fingerprint work. "He saw Scotland Yard men taking fingerprints at Liverpool and [he] began studying the science." After the war, he continued to pursue his interest in fingerprinting as a hobby while serving as a member of the medical advisory board of the Federal Trade Commission. He had also been running his own medical practice in New York since 1923.

Hudson became an expert in the study of fingerprints and fingerprinting techniques and in July 1935 Police Commissioner Lewis Valeninte appointed him an honorary consultant to the New York Police Department.

Doctor Hudson was called to testify at many criminal trials, the most famous being that of Richard Hauptmann in early 1935. He was called by the Defense to testify on Hauptmann's behalf. "Using a nitrate of silver process, [Hudson] testified he had found hundreds of prints on the ladder used in the kidnapping" where the State Police had found none. Not one of the prints found matched Hauptmann's.

Later that year, he "turned over his process for identifying prints to the New York Police Department...It enabled the department to abandon the old powder-dusting system. The new system brings out prints on materials other than those with smooth surfaces."

Doctor Hudson died in Washington, D. C. on September 17, 1943 at Mount Alto hospital after suffering a long illness. He was only 55 years old.

It is probably quite safe to say that very few people at the trial of Richard Hauptmann had ever heard of a Xylotomist, but he was one of the most damning witnesses called to take the witness stand. His testimony remains very controversial today, with one group of people saying that his research with out a doubt connects Richard Hauptmann to the kidnapping and another group saying that he proved little or nothing. His findings and subsequent testimony are hotly debated in just about every book written on the Hauptmann Trial and the reader is directed to any of the books to learn more about this controversial figure's testimony. Just look in the index under "Koehler, Arthur."

Arthur Koehler, the aptly dubbed "wood expert" from the Hauptmann Trial was born on a farm near Manitowoc, Wisconsin in 1886. He attended Lawrence College at Appleton for two years and then graduated from the University of Michigan School of Forestry in 1911. While there, he was able to teach classes on wood identification.

After graduating from Michigan, he joined the United States Department of Agriculture's Forest Service. In 1914 he transferred to the Forest Products Laboratory as a *xylotomist* – a wood structure specialist. His research there "led to the establishment of the division of silvicultural relations...whose main function was research on the structure and growth of wood in trees under various conditions of soil, light, rainfall and cultural practices such as pruning and tree spacing."

In 1932 when it became known that the ladder used in the Lindbergh kidnapping was a home made wooden ladder, Koehler contacted the New Jersey State Police to offer his services. The State Police had not called him because, in 1932, they had never even heard of a *xylotomist*!

Koehler examined the kidnap ladder and worked closely with Detective Lewis Bornmann as they searched for the source of its wood. At one point, while driving through the Bronx, Koehler had suggested searching Dr Condon's house and garage to see if either of them could have been the source of the ladder wood. After all, Condon was deeply involved in the case as the go-between and was always looked upon with suspicion by the police. However, after Hauptmann's arrest in September 1934 and Bornmann's discovery of a floorboard in his attic that had been cut short, Koehler was able to match the attic flooring (known as *S-226*) with one of the ladder's side rails (known as *Rail 16*). This match, through very controversial among many researchers of the Lindbergh Case today, was one of the many pieces of forensic evidence that helped to convince the jury to find Hauptmann guilty.

After the Hauptmann trial, Koehler returned to his laboratory in Madison, Wisconsin where he "contributed to the solution of many wood utilization problems. During the Second World War, for example, "he applied his science to alleviating shortages of war materials…from aircraft to gunstocks…and artificial limbs for disabled fighting men."

Koehler retired from the Forest Products Laboratory's Division of Silvercultural Relations in 1948. He and his first wife moved to Los Angeles where he taught courses on wood structure and properties for the University of California at Los Angeles Extension Service. He also taught at the University of British Columbia and at Yale for two years.

Koehler's first wife died in 1950 and he remarried in 1951. He died sixteen years later in Los Angeles after suffering a long illness on July 17, 1967 at age 82. He is buried at the Forest Lawn Memorial Park in Hollywood Hills, California.

A portion of his collection of articles and other materials relating to the Lindbergh Case are on file at the New Jersey State Police Museum and Learning Center in West Trenton, New Jersey. His scrapbook from the Hauptmann Trial is on file at the New Jersey State Archives in Trenton. A collection of his photographs is also on file with the United States Forest Products Laboratory in Madison, Wisconsin.

Eight experts in the field of questioned document examination were called to testify at the trial of Richard Hauptmann in 1935. The principal expert called on to examine both the handwriting in the ransom notes as well as that of potential suspects was Albert S. Osborn, the dean of the art of questioned document examination.

Born in 1858 in Sharon, Michigan, Albert Osborn was educated in local public schools. He had no college degree until he received an honorary doctorate from Colby College in 1938. Osborn began studying handwriting examination in 1887 and in 1910 he opened his own office.

A member of the Phi Delta Theta fraternity as well as the Masons, he published two editions of *Questioned Documents, The Problem of Proof, The Mind of the Juror* and *Questioned Document Problems*, which he co-authored with his son Albert D. Osborn.

Since his firm was originally in Montclair, New Jersey the State Police often called on him for consultations. By the time he testified at the Hauptmann Trial he had over thirty years' experience as an expert witness on questioned handwriting "and had done so in thirty-nine states and various parts of Canada and Puerto Rico." He also worked on a case in London that had originally been sent to him from New Zealand.

Osborn charged the State of New Jersey $12,000 for his expert services during the Lindbergh investigation. The Attorney General, David Wilentz said that it was justified because Osborn had "served the State in the very highest and most capable manner."

Albert S. Osborn lived in Montclair, New Jersey. He died at home on December 15, 1946 when he was 88 years old.

His son, Albert D. Osborn, was a senior partner in the family business. Born in 1896 in Rochester, New York, he attended college at Dartmouth. In 1914 he enlisted in the French Army to fight in the First World War and, once the United States became involved in 1917 he joined the American forces.

Albert D. worked with his father in the family business and was the past president of the American Society of Questioned Document Examiners, an organization his father had started in 1942.

He testified at the Hauptmann Trial and concurred with his father – and the other expert witnesses – that Richard Hauptmann had indeed written all fifteen ransom notes. Forty years later, he was involved in another high profile questioned handwriting case.

In 1971 he "first declared valid and then declared a forgery handwriting alleged to be that of Howard Hughes in connection with Clifford Irving's fraudulent autobiography of Mr. Hughes." Osborn explained at that time that the art of questioned document examination "is not an exact science" and in the case of the "really beautiful forgeries" of Howard Hughes, "somebody really did a lot of spade work."

Albert D. Osborn and his family lived near his father in Montclair, New Jersey. He died at the Mountainside Hospital in Glen Ridge on October 28, 1972 at the age of 76.

Forensic psychology was another new field utilized by police investigators in the early part of the twentieth century. Originally known as alienists, psychiatrists helped the police by analyzing the crime and evidence, such as ransom correspondence, left behind by the criminal in an attempt to paint a picture, so to speak, of whoever it was the police were after.

Doctor Dudley D. Schoenfeld was one such pioneering psychiatrist who often consulted with the New York City Police as a criminal profiler. He was brought into the Lindbergh Case by Lieutenant Finn of the New York Police and asked to provide a profile of the kidnapper based on an analysis of the ransom notes. In 1936 he published "The Crime and the Criminal", the only psychiatric study of the Lindbergh Case.

Born in 1893, Schoenfeld received his medical degree in 1917 from New York University's medical school. He then served in the United States Navy as a physician during the remainder of the First World War and it was at this time that he developed an interest in psychology.

Once the war was over, Schoenfeld joined the American Psychiatric Association and the American Psychoanalytic Association. He was also a charter member of the New York Psychoanalytic Society. While working at Mount Sinai Hospital, he established the first mental health clinic in New York City.

During the Second World War, he was appointed to the board of psychiatrists who screened the applicants for the Women's Army Auxiliary Corps. Schoenfeld was also a member of the LaGuardia Commission that conducted "a study of the marijuana problem" in Manhattan and in 1944 released a report that "marijuana was not much more addictive than cigarettes."

Dudley Schoenfeld died on September 27, 1971 at Mount Sinai Hospital where he was once chief psychiatrist. His wife, the former Helen Frankenstein, survived him.

Regardless of the controversy that continues to surround the forensic evidence of the Hauptmann Trial, it must be acknowledged that these men, and others like them, who testified at the Hauptmann trial were among the founding fathers of forensic science and forensic expert testimony. What is now commonplace in courtrooms across the country was, at the time of Hauptmann's trial, considered new and obscure, especially to the jurors of rural Hunterdon County. While not as sophisticated as today's forensic investigators, these men paved the way for what has become the lynchpin of many modern court cases around the world.

23. C. Lloyd Fisher

It is not very often that the assisting attorney at a trial becomes more popular and well known than the lead attorney, but in the case of C. Lloyd Fisher of the Hauptmann defense team, it should not be very surprising. Lloyd Fisher was a very popular attorney in Flemington and many felt that he should have been Hauptmann's primary defense lawyer. He was, after all, the only one who really believed their client was not guilty. That was something about which Fisher never changed his mind. He believed the execution was "'the greatest tragedy in the history of New Jersey...[something] time will never wash out.'" Shortly before he died Fisher said, 'the passing years have only served to convince me more firmly than ever that a great misjustice [sic] occurred when Hauptmann was executed."

Fisher was born on September 27, 1896 in Raritan Township on the "old Flemington Water Company farm" just off Route 12 near the township border. His parents, William V. Fisher and Margaret Lake Fisher moved to Flemington when he was a child. Lloyd lived there for the rest of his life, attending local public schools before going off fight in World War I.

After the war he attended Dickinson Law School at Carlisle, Pennsylvania graduating in 1923. In 1924 he was admitted to the New Jersey Bar and he then began his practice in Flemington in partnership with C. Raymon Herre. In 1925 he married Eda Williamson, the 28-year-old daughter of Frank T. and Adarenna Tindale Williamson of Elizabeth, New Jersey. In 1929 they purchased their home at 34 Maple Avenue in Flemington where they spent the rest of their lives together.

The fact that the very personable Lloyd Fisher was very active in Flemington both athletically and civically contributed to his popularity. "He was a smooth dancer [and] a handy man with a pool cue." He enjoyed sports, especially "...cycling, wrestling and boxing [and he] was an amateur tennis champion."

He kept in touch with his fellow veterans and served as Vice Commander of the Flemington Post of the American Legion. He also served as the president of the Hunterdon County Bar Association and then as its secretary for twenty years and the Flemington National Bank and Trust Company took him on as their director.

Fisher liked to drive fast and would even dare the police to try to catch him. He did get caught on occasion, as he did on July 3, 1937 when he was "driving fifty miles an hour in Union County." Motorcycle patrolman William Dierolf pulled him over and issued a ticket. Fisher appeared in court on July 29th where he entered a plea of "justifiable speeding." He went on to explain that he was "hurrying to New York City to keep an important engagement having to do with a criminal investigation and the delay caused him to miss the appointment." He did not begrudge the police officer and "complimented [him] for halting him, but said he thought he might have used 'a little more judgment in the matter.'" The charge against him was later dismissed.

Lloyd Fisher was involved with the Lindbergh Case long before anyone ever heard of Bruno Richard Hauptmann. During the summer of 1932 he was the defense attorney for John Hughes Curtis, the man accused of perpetrating a hoax against Colonel Lindbergh in which he claimed to be in contact with the kidnappers. Three years later, because of his popularity in Flemington, he was brought on board Hauptmann's defense team as Edward J. Reilly's assistant. It was Fisher who presented the defense's opening argument at the trial and it was also Fisher who jumped up and hollered, "You have just condemned this man to the electric chair" and stormed out of the courtroom when Reilly conceded that the corpse found in the woods near Hopewell was the body of Charles Lindbergh, Jr.

During the trial, reporters noted, "Mr. Fisher scribbles on a tablet of legal foolscap. He writes his name, C. Lloyd Fisher, over and over. According to the local newspaper, Mr. Fisher was known as Lloyd Fisher before the trial began. Now he is C. Lloyd Fisher. Of the defense lawyers, he is the most elegant."

According to court stenographers, Fisher was the "fastest talker among the attorneys at the Hauptmann Trial." Close behind in second place was David Wilentz, the Attorney General. Fisher "sometimes uttered 300 words a minute. His total, if he had a fast-talking witness [on the stand] would make a full-length novel each day."

After the trial ended, the Hauptmanns fired Reilly and appointed Fisher as their chief counsel to handle the appeal. Fisher filed that appeal on May

10, 1935 in which he cited 193 points of law that he felt justified a reversal of the conviction as well as a new trial. He presented oral arguments before the Court of Errors and Appeal on June 20th but it was not until October 9th that the fourteen judges of the Appeal court unanimously voted to affirm Hauptmann's conviction.

On May 24, 1937 Governor Harold G. Hoffman nominated Fisher to replace Anthony Hauck, Jr. as Hunterdon County Prosecutor. Hauck, one of the prosecutors at the Hauptmann Trial, had left office on April 27th when his five-year term expired. Before Fisher, an attorney-at-law could be nominated, the State Legislature had to pass a bill "exempting fourth class counties from the statutory requirement that prosecutors be counselors-at-law" which they did just prior to the Governor announcing the nomination.

When word first got out in February that the Governor wanted to nominate him, Lloyd Fisher "belittled reports that his appointment to the office might lead to a re-opening of the Lindbergh baby kidnap-murder case." He said that "there's nothing about that office that in any manner, shape or form could revive the Hauptmann Case...there's nothing in the Hunterdon County Office about the case I don't [already] know."

Fisher's nomination was confirmed by the state Senate and he held the office of prosecutor for one term. After leaving office in 1942, he went back to his law practice and served as legal counsel to Colonel Arthur Foran, the State Milk Control Director. He and Foran had adjoining properties in West Amwell Township that had several lakes on them. They made the land available to the Boy Scouts who dubbed it "Camp Foran-Fisher."

During the 1950s, Lloyd Fisher was diagnosed with cancer. He received extensive treatments and endured several operations as he tried unsuccessfully to combat the horrible disease. He lost his battle at the Clifford Springs, New York Sanatorium where he died on July 1, 1960 at the age of 63.

Not surprisingly there was standing room only at the Holcombe Funeral Home on Main Street in Flemington where his funeral was held. Reverend Homer Watson Henderson, the pastor of the Flemington Methodist Church where Fisher was an active member, officiated at his funeral. Reverend Henderson paid tribute to his "dynamic personality" reminding everyone that Fisher was "ever at the forefront of events which during the years of his professional activity brought vast changes in the community, the county, the state and nation."

Eda, Lloyd Fisher's wife of 35 years, survived him by forty-one years. She died in Flemington on October 15, 2001 at the age of 104.

24. Frederick Pope

Frederick Allan Pope was one of the last attorneys to join Hauptmann's defense team. Rumors had circulated for several weeks prior to him being retained on December 5, 1934 to assist Edward J. Reilly.

Pope had three conditions that had to be met before he would accept the position. First, he had to be assured he would be paid. He also had to be assured that his fee would not be paid from the ransom money! And lastly, the evidence held by the defense had to be enough to substantiate a "reasonably good case" for their client. Demands such as these make it very easy to believe that not everyone on the defense team believed in their client's innocence.

Frederick Pope of Somerville, New Jersey was born in 1872. From 1905 to 1910 he was the Assistant Prosecutor of Somerset County and Prosecutor from 1910 to 1915. During this time, in January 1914, he was involved in the case of Paul Carl, a young man from East Stroudsburg, Pennsylvania who, in November 1911, "fired a load of buckshot" into the back of Monroe F. Ellis, president of the Conkling Lumber Company. He claimed he was hired by a woman to kill Ellis for $400.

Later, Pope opened his own law practice and in 1925 unsuccessfully defended Daniel Genese who was later convicted of murdering Trooper Robert Coyle the previous December. Trooper Coyle was the first New Jersey State Trooper to be murdered in the line of duty. On December 18, 1924, at about 5:00 P. M., Troopers John Gregovesir and Robert Coyle were escorting Genese, an attempted payroll robbery suspect, to the Pluckemin Substation for questioning. The two troopers sat in the front seat, leaving the suspect unattended in the back seat. While driving along the highway near Chimney Rock, adjacent to Bound Brook in Somerset County, the suspect suddenly shouted "Hands Up!" Trooper Coyle, who was riding in the passenger seat, turned and the man fired a blank directly into Coyle's face. The man then wrested Coyle's revolver from him and fired two shots into Trooper Coyle's back. Trooper Coyle died immediately.

During the last day of Genese's trial, Pope made a sarcastic comment regarding a Lieutenant Druen, a Jersey City Police fingerprint expert. It had caused such a commotion in the courtroom that the judge finally had to clear the room of its 500 spectators and remind them that the murder trial was a serious matter. Genese was found guilty and later executed in the same electric chair as Richard Hauptmann.

Frederick Pope was very prominent in Republican politics in Somerset County and just prior to the commencement of the Hauptmann Trial he was nominated as the District Court Judge of Somerset County. His nomination was confirmed an in March 1935 he was sworn in as judge.

Pope was very active in local civic organization. He was a high-ranking member of the Masons and the past state president of both the Elks and the Knights of Pythias. He was also the former national president of the Patriotic Sons of America.

Frederick Pope was married but had no children. He died on June 22, 1952 at the age of 80.

25. Egbert Rosecrans

Tall, thin and distinguished looking, Egbert Rosecrans of Warren County was born in 1890 in Hoboken, New Jersey. He was a direct descendant of Harmon Rosecrans, a Dutch immigrant who had settled in New Amsterdam in 1657.

In the early 1920s, Rosecrans was the Warren County Counsel and worked out of his office in Blairstown. He caused a bit of a stir in the county when the *New York Times* ran a story on November 1, 1923 where they reported that he had been "arrested on a charge of atrocious assault and his clerk Samuel T. Beatty, for aiding and abetting in the assault."

Mr. and Mrs. Frederick S. Brooks of New York City preferred the charges wherein they claimed that when they and their son Harold went to Rosecrans' office "in reference to a statement which they alleged was made by Rosecrans reflecting on Mrs. Brooks' character, Rosecrans and his clerk forcibly ejected them from the office." Nothing substantial came of these charges. Rosecrans rejected their offer of an out-of-court settlement, preferring to face them in open court. He continued in his position in Warren County eventually becoming a Warren County Court judge. He held that position until his death on January 20, 1948.

26. Anthony Hauck, Jr.

Anthony Hauck had just recently been appointed to his five-year term as Hunterdon County Prosecutor when the Lindbergh Kidnapping occurred in 1932 and in 1935 he was called on to assist Attorney General David Wilentz with his prosecution of the most famous case the county had ever tried – that of Bruno Richard Hauptmann.

Hauck came to Flemington in 1928 from nearby Somerville. He was, however, a native of Jersey City where he was born in 1901 to Anthony and Eliza Moffatt Hauck. He attended Wesleyan University and the New Jersey School of Law (now Rutgers School of Law). Upon graduating in 1928 he was admitted to the state bar worked in Clinton with the firm Gebhardt and Gebhardt. He opened his own practice in 1931 in partnership with J. Knox Felter. Later, when Felter was elected surrogate he went into partnership with Wesley L. Lance. In 1935, at the time of the Lindbergh trial, he was the senior partner in the law firm of Hauck and McIntyre in Clinton.

Hauck had served in the State Assembly from 1931 to 1932 in Clinton, resigning when he was appointed County Prosecutor. The town of Clinton was very Republican yet Hauck, a Democrat, "was able to carry the town by 443 to 19 votes." Eventually he became Democratic Party's county chairman in Hunterdon.

For forty-four years, Hauck practiced law spending thirty-five of them in Hunterdon County where he served as counsel to municipalities and school boards. He belonged to many legal and civic organizations including the boy scouts, the Masons and Kiwanis. He also headed the March of Dimes in Hunterdon County and served on Huntedon's Selective Service advisory board.

In 1957 Hauck's 15-year-old daughter, Sandra, was involved in a strange shooting that took place in their Flemington home. According to an April

5, 1957, *New York Times* article, Anthony Hauck was the general counsel of the Idaho Uranium and Thorium Mining Company. The shooting victim, 52-year-old Dr. Thomas Stoelting of Salmon, Idaho, was a mining engineer and an executive of the company. Stoelting and Hauck were involved in the "speculative mining venture" along with Rolf Meuer, and others. It was Rolf's gun that Sandra used in the shooting. According to court documents,

> For some six years prior to the shooting Stoelting stayed as a guest in the Hauck home on numerous occasions and often for extended periods of time. During the six months before the shooting, he stayed there one or two nights a week. On the evening of April 2, 1957, there was a business conference at the Hauck home. Afterwards, Stoelting and Anthony Hauck, Jr., had a conversation in the dining room on the first floor. During the conversation, Stoelting said (of his wife, according to his testimony), 'she has had her last chance to save her neck. 'Sandra had already gone up to her bedroom on the second floor, but she apparently overheard Stoelting's remark, and interpreted it as a threat to her mother. At about one o'clock, Stoelting and Hauck went upstairs to the bedroom they shared, and retired to their separate beds. Sandra, according to her answers to interrogatories, which were read to the jury, took a gun from an unlocked desk in her room, thinking it unloaded. She entered the room occupied by Stoelting and her father, and walked to the foot of Stoelting's bed. She asked him whether he had been talking about her mother. Before he answered she 'pulled the gun up in order to frighten him and it suddenly went off.'

Stoelting was taken to the Hunterdon County Medical Center for treatment. While there, he was served with an arrest warrant on "morals charges" involving Sandra Hauck. On May 9th, allegations were made that

> between September 1955 and May 1956 Stoelting 'physically and mentally assaulted' Sandra, in an automobile, in and about her home, and in a nearby barn or outbuilding. His alleged assaults occurred 'two, three or four times a week,' and consisted of having sexual intercourse with her, striking her, attempting to indulge in unnatural sex acts with her, and threatening to beat and injure her and to kill her parents if she told them about his actions. It was also alleged that...he

applied and supplied to this defendant various drugs which further destroyed the emotional and mental capacity of the defendant, Sandra Hauck, making it impossible for her to resist'; and that he continued to 'mentally abuse, coerce and threaten' Sandra up to the date of the shooting. The cumulative effect of Stoelting's actions was alleged to be such that 'coupled with the threat of the plaintiff which she had heard that evening, it disturbed her mentally and emotionally to such a degree that she has no recollection of pulling the trigger or causing the gun to be discharged, although…she did intend to scare him…

A twenty-four hour guard was immediately placed on his room. At the same time, Sandra Hauck was charged with juvenile delinquency. She was ruled a juvenile delinquent "…after a two-and-one-half-hour hearing before Judge Harry Z. Lindeman of the Essex County Juvenile and Domestic Relations Court." On October 11th, however, Dr. Stoelting was acquitted of the abuse charges.

Thomas Stoelting survived the shooting and sued the Hauck family for negligence. A jury awarded him $100,000 in damages. He eventually moved to Fairbanks, Alaska where he died in May 1984.

Anthony Hauck, Jr., Hunterdon County's most noted and admired lawyer, died suddenly of a heart attack on September 13, 1972 when he was just 71 years old. The Flemington courtroom where his memorial service was held was filled with colleagues wishing to pay him tribute. David Wilentz was one of the principal speakers. They knew each other from before the Hauptmann trial, "right from the beginning of his practice."

"They say the good die young. I say that whenever a good man dies, he's too young. Besides being a good and respected lawyer, he was a good man, simple, wholesome, delightful. Tony was a warm person."

Anthony Hauck is buried in Mountain View Cemetery in Cokesbury, New Jersey.

Notes

1. Reprinted from the New Jersey State Police Teacher's Guide, 1994.
2. Reprinted from *In The Footsteps of Red Johnson* by Mark W. Falzini, 2003.

3. The following account of Red's activities until his arrest are, for the most part, in his own words, taken from his March 8, 1932 statement to the police.

4. The Lindberghs had spent the weekend in Hopewell and the baby came down with a cold. Mrs. Lindbergh decided to break with routine and stay over an additional night. When she awoke on Tuesday, she, too, had developed a cold. She called Englewood and requested that Betty come down to Hopewell to help care for the baby while she rested.

5. The Court Confectionary Store at 32 Van Brunt Street, in Englewood.

6. Actually 8:30 pm.

7. Ironically, $50,000 was also the amount paid in ransom by Charles Lindbergh just three months earlier.

8. This is from Chrystal Lee Möller's thesis: The Law of Jante in Swedish Society. (University of Minnesota, 1998). This is a fascinating dissertation on the Jante Law as it applies to Swedish and Scandinavian culture in general. It can be found at http://www.waste.org/~xtal/red/jante.html.

9. The "musical evenings" was Richard Hauptmann's alibi for Saturday, April 2, 1932 when he was accused of meeting with Dr. John Condon in Woodlawn Cemetery and receiving the ransom payment. However, the Hauptmanns had no gas or electric that night. According to a report

filed by Detective Claude Patterson of the New Jersey State Police dated
October 1, 1934, Mr. W.G. Peterson, the Credit Manager of the Bronx
Gas and Electric Company advised him that Hauptmann's landlord, "Max
Rausch…requested that their meter service be discontinue[d], March 29,
1932" and Hauptmann made application "…for reopening [on] April 4,
1932."

[10] For more on his involvement with what he referred to as "The Great Case,"
it is recommended that the reader seek out any of the books already written
on the Lindbergh Case or, for the adventurous, to examine the original
police reports on file at the New Jersey State Police Museum archive.

[11] Copies of these books are on file at both the Library of Congress and the
NJ State Police Museum.

[12] Many people confuse this medal with the Congressional Medal of Honor.
The "Gold Lifesaving Medal" was established by an Act of Congress on
June 20, 1874 and is awarded by the Commandant of the Coast Guard
"…to any person who rescues, or endeavors to rescue, any other person from
drowning, shipwreck, or other peril of the water. To merit [the] award…the
rescue must be made at the risk to one's own life and show extreme heroic
daring…"

[13] The Matthews Construction Company, Inc. was a general contractor
located in Princeton, New Jersey. They had worked on such buildings as
the Princeton University Store and the neo-Gothic University Chapel. They
also worked on buildings at Cornel University in Ithica. W.R. Matthews,
who hired stonemasons from Scotland "for economic reasons", founded
it and they employed an apprentice system where everyone hired "was
trained in the Scottish way of handling the stone." The company went out
of business in 1968.

[14] There are several stories regarding famous people who stayed in the
various guest rooms of the house, such as Presidents Coolidge, Hoover
and Roosevelt, FBI Director J. Edgar Hoover, Albert Einstein and others.
These are urban legends, stories that when looked at historically make little
sense.

[15] Probably around 1921 or 1922

[16] 1914-1918

[17] The Rt. Hon. Lord Islington, PC KCMG DSO (John Dixon Poynder) was
Governor of New Zealand from January 1910 through December 1912;
Undersecretary of State for India in 1913 and a member of the House of

Lords who spoke in flavor of granting women the right to vote in England and, in 1923, spoke in opposition to the Balfour Declaration.

[18] Delirium Tremens, commonly known, as "the DTs" is a potentially fatal condition caused by alcohol withdrawal and is common in heavy drinkers and alcoholics.

[19] A New York Times article dated February 18, 1947 states that they had been separated for three years, making the date of separation 1944. A March 28, 1947 Times article lists the date as July 2, 1940.

[20] This is now Christ and St. Luke's Church, Norfolk.

[21] See: Archival Ramblings: *Mission to Iran*. http://njspmuseum.blogspot.com/2007/03/mission-to-iran_120.html.

[22] Reprinted from the author's blog, Archival Ramblings. *Hugo Stockburger 1906 - 2007: Zum Gedächtnis eines großen Mannes*. Http://njspmuseum.blogspot.com/2007/06/hugo-stockburger-1906-2007.html. June 21, 2007.

[23] Due to the fiscal crises caused by the Great Depression, no classes occurred during this time. The last class was held during the summer of 1931 and the next one did not occur until the summer of 1938.

[24] The State Police divides New Jersey into administrative sections called Troops. Troop "A" covers southern New Jersey. Troop "B" covers the northern part of the state and Troop "C", which was created in the early 1930s, covers central New Jersey. Two additional troops, "D" and "E" were added in the 1950s. In the 1930s a "Troop Commander" held the rank of Captain.

[25] Interview by author with retired Major Hugo Stockburger, January 21, 2005.

[26] Please see chapter on Hugo Stockburger.

[27] Also named Arthur and Lydia

[28] Robert Peacock was one of the assistant prosecutors during the Hauptmann Trial.

[29] It should be noted that the Social Security Death Database lists his birth date as May 2, 1897.

[30] He married Susan Berish on October 25, 1930.

[31] From 1921 until 1948, when the government of the State of New Jersey was reorganized, the State Police was a Department and its headquarters was

located on West State Street in Trenton, across the street from the Capital. After reorganization, it was reduced to a Division under the Department of Law and Public Safety (where it remains today) and the headquarters was moved to the Wilburtha training school, now known as West Trenton.

[32] He, too, was issued the Distinguished Service Award for his work in the Lindbergh Case investigation.

[33] Not to be confused with Joseph McCarthy's anti-Communist hearings in the Senate.

[34] The company was originally known as The Germania Fire Insurance Company and was one of the oldest insurance companies in the country, having been founded in 1859. In 1918 it changed it's name to the National Liberty Insurance Company of America because of "the public misinterpretation of the former name, which it was said led many to believe that the company was German in its origin or affiliation." This was a perception the company wanted to avoid once the United States became involved in the First World War.

[35] Coincidentally, when he divorced Loretta in 1941, he hired C. Lloyd Fisher, who had been Richard Hauptmann's defense attorney, to serve as his divorce counsel.

[36] Dr. Carter G. Woodson, the "Father of Black History" who established Black History Week and later Black History Month was born in Buckingham County in 1875.

[37] Her name is often misspelled as Sharpe in Lindbergh Kidnapping related literature and even some original police reports. Her original birth certificate as well as documents pertaining to her family in England and even her own signature shows that the correct spelling is Sharp.

[38] Some books about the Lindbergh Case mention that Violet was promiscuous and possibly even pregnant when she died. Other than a single report referencing a possible liaison with a man named William O'Brien, these assertions are not supported by archival documentation.

[39] Emily went by the name Edna while in the United States.

[40] The Morrow summer home in North Haven, Maine. Her mother had written to her that her "eyes keep so bad I can hardly see anything at times" and her father tended to drink to much and was a rather argumentative drunk. Lucy Sharp lived for another nine years after Violet's suicide. She died on January 18, 1941 in Salisbury from acute bronchitis.

⁴¹ "Oyer and Terminer" is from Anglo-French and simply means "to hear and to determine."

⁴² Robbins had also presided over the infamous John Hughes Curtis "Hoax" trial in 1932.

⁴³ For a discussion on the conduct of the trial, the reader is directed to any of the myriad of books on the subject of the Lindbergh Kidnapping, with special attention given to "The Lindbergh Kidnapping Case: The Trial of Bruno Richard Hauptmann" by Sydney Whipple, "The Airman and The Carpenter" by Ludovic Kennedy, and "The Case That Never Dies" by Lloyd Gardner.

⁴⁴ Harold Nicolson was a British diplomat and author who had met Lindbergh in 1933 when he was commissioned to write Dwight Morrow's biography. The Lindberghs stayed at Nicolson's estate when they moved to England in 1936.

⁴⁵ Located on East Hanover and North Montgomery Streets in Trenton

⁴⁶ The Taylor Wharton Iron and Steel Company had been in existence from 1742 until it finally shut down in 1972. It was the oldest iron and steel company in the United States and it had provided armaments for all of the wars of the United States. It had also supplied machinery for the construction of the Panama Canal.

⁴⁷ They were later divorced.

Suggested Reading

This book is not meant to be a book specifically about the Lindbergh Kidnapping and subsequent trial of Bruno Richard Hauptmann. Rather, it is a book about the people that have been forever trapped by the Crime and Trial of the Century. The collection biographical essays that are found here is an attempt to paint a broader picture of these people that are forever linked to the "great case."

Therefore, it is recommended that this book be read in conjunction with any of the others about the Lindbergh Case in which the subjects of this book will be found. The following list is but a small sampling of the many books and articles that are available about the Lindbergh Kidnapping Case and Hauptmann Trial.

Fisher, Jim. *The Lindbergh Case.* Rutgers University Press, New Brunswick, 1987.

Gardner, Lloyd C. *The Case That Never Dies.* Rutgers University Press, New Brunswick. 2004.

Kennedy, Ludovic. "The Airman and the Carpenter." Viking Press, 1985.

Milton, Joyce. "Loss of Eden." Harper Collins, NY. 1993.

Waller, George. *Kidnap: The Story of the Lindbergh Case.* Dial, Publishers, NY. 1961

Sources

1. Red Johnson

"On the Sunny Side of the Oslofjord." Moss og Omegn TouristSenter.

Bureau of Investigation Summary Report. February 1934.

Corsi, Edward. Commissioner of Immigration. Letter to Konrad Furubotn, US Department of Labor, July 20, 1932.

Gow, Betty. Trial Transcripts. State of New Jersey v. Bruno Richard Hauptmann.

Johansen, Else Marie. Interview with author. October 4, 2003.

Johansen, Fin Henrik. Letter to Sigurd Arnesen, Nordisk Tidende, July 28, 1932

Johansen, Fin Henrik. Statement. March 15, 1932

Johansen, Fin Henrik. Statement. March 8, 1932.

London Times. March 7, 1932.

McGrath, Sergeant. Letter to Frank Brex, Newark Police Department. March 12, 1932.

Möller, Chrystal Lee. The Law of Jante in Swedish Society. Thesis. University of Minnesota, 1998.

New York Times, March 5, 1932.

New York Times, March 13, 1932.

New York Times, March 19, 1932.

Nordisk Tidende, July 28, 1932.

Vinje, Tor. Interview with author. October 3, 2003.

Winterhalter, Charles (NYPD). Grand Jury Minutes. "People v. John Doe." June 1932.

2. Hauptmann's Car

Dodge Brothers Motor Vehicle Order Form, March 3, 1931

Horn, Cpl. William F. "Report of investigation concerning search of Dodge Sedan…" R1600. September 26, 1934.

Kennedy, Ludovic. "The Airman and the Carpenter." Viking Press, 1985.

Lyle, Walter. Statement. September 22, 1934.

Lyons, John Joseph. Statement. September 22, 1934.

Hauptmann, Bruno Richard. Motor Vehicle Registration. 1931

Hauptmann, Bruno Richard. Motor Vehicle Registration. 1932

Hauptmann, Bruno Richard. Motor Vehicle Registration. 1933

Hauptmann, Bruno Richard. Motor Vehicle Registration. 1934

New York Sun, April 15, 1937

Report of Motor Vehicle Accident. Richard Hauptmann and Alexander Begg. October 17, 1932.

Trenton Evening Times, January 11, 1943

Williamsbridge Motors, Inc. Invoice No 001, March 9, 1931

Zapolsky, Trooper Andrew. "Report of continued investigation concerning Bruno

Richard Hauptmann, re: Lindbergh Case." R1600. November 10, 1934.

3. Hans Kloppenburg

Kennedy, Ludovic. "The Airman and the Carpenter." Viking Press, 1985.

Kloppenburg, Hans. Obituary. Asbury Park Press. January 5, 1989

Kloppenburg, Hans. Social Security Death Database. http://ssdi. genealogy. rootsweb. com/

Kloppenburg, Hans. Statement. 10/8/1934.

Kloppenburg, Hans. Testimony. State of New Jersey vs. Bruno Richard Hauptmann Trial Transcripts. 1935.

Patterson, Det. Claude. "Investigation of Gas and Electric Accounts of Bruno Richard Hauptmann." R1600. October 1, 1934.

4. Attorney General David T. Wilentz

Mitchell, Joseph. M. "Crier Calls Terminer 'Terminal' And Judge Gets His Daily Laugh." World-Telegram. January 30, 1935. (Miller Scrapbook #13)

New Jersey Office of the Attorney General. Biographies www. state. nj. us/ lps/oag/ag_1934-1944_wilentz_bio. htm

University of Missouri-Kansas. "Famous American Trials" www. law. umkc. edu/faculty/projects/ftrials/Hauptmann/wilentz. html

Wilentz, David T. Find A Grave. www. findagrave. com

Wilentz, David T. Obituary. Atlantic City Press. July 7, 1988

Wilentz, David T. Obituary. Boston Globe. July 7, 1988

Wilentz, David T. Obituary. New York Times. July 7, 1988

Wilentz, David T. Social Security Death Database. http://ssdi.genealogy. rootsweb.com/

5. Robert Peacock

Peacock, Robert. Brief Biographical Statement. Unknown Source.

Peacock, Robert. Obituary. 1955.

6. Jafsie

"Gold Lifesaving Medal." www. foxfall. com/fmd-uscg-glsm. htm

"Patty Doyle's Family & The Lindbergh Case." www. rense. com/general74/ doyle. htm

Condon, John F. Obituary. New York Times. January 2, 1945.

Condon, John F. Testimony. State of New Jersey vs. Bruno Richard Hauptmann

Report #375, October 27, 1934 by Thomas H. Sisk re: Condon's scrapbooks. Trial Transcripts. 1935.

7. Hans & Maria Müller

Breed, P. M. and J. S. Kavanaugh, Special Agents. FBI62-3057. "Memorandum For the File." R1600. September 21, 1934.

Hartman, Patricia. Correspondence. December 2007

Haussling, DSG Eugene A. "Guard at home of B. Richard Hauptmann, 1279 East 222nd Street, Bronx, New York." R1600. September 19, 1934.

Haussling, DSG Eugene A. "Apprehension of and search of apartment of Hans Mueller 2701 Marion Ave., Bronx, NY." R1600. September 20, 1934.

Kelly, DSG W. P. "Investigation of the Lindbergh Case in New York City re: Radiola at the home of Hans Mueller, 2601[sic] Marion St., New York City." R1600. September 1934.

Kelly, DSG W. P. "Investigation of the Lindbergh Case in New York City re: Payment Made by Hans Mueller to Dr. Jos. S. Brandstein, 2952 Marion Ave., New York City." R1600. October 2, 1934.

Kennedy, Ludovic. The Airman and the Carpenter. Viking Press, 1985.

Leon, Cpl. Samuel J. "Investigation of Frank Lewinski, Clason Point, Bronx, New York Who recommended Hans Mueller to Henry Reimer for a job on the boat "Marquita", re: report of Sgt. Zapolsky dated November 15, 1934." R1600. November 21, 1934.

Leon, Cpl. Samuel J. "Investigation of Frank Lewinski, Clason Point, Bronx, New York Re: report of November 21, 1934 and November 22, 1934." R1600. November 22, 1934.

Leon, Cpl. Samuel J. "Continuing investigation on Frank Lewinsky, Clason Point, Bronx, New York re: report of November 28, 1934." R1600. November 30, 1934.

Müller, Maria. Obituary. Mobile Register. March 25, 1999.

Müller, Hans and Maria. Statements. October 11, 1934. District Attorney's Office, Bronx County, New York.

Zapolsky, Sgt. Andrew. "Continued investigation re: Bruno Richard Hauptmann, re: Lindbergh Case." R1600. November 13, 1934.

Zapolsky, Sgt. Andrew. "Continued report of investigation with reference to Bruno Richard Hauptmann, re: Lindbergh Case." R1600. November 15, 1934.

8. Highfields

"Griffing Made Drawings for Matthews Blueprints." The Princeton Recollector. August 1981.

"Hotel Will Be Completed by September 1937 Entire Project Before 1941." The Princeton Recollector. Autumn 1978.

"Little Fire Evoked Memories of Gymnasium Debacle." The Princeton Recollector. June 1980.

"Margerum Recalls Painstaking Reassembly of Colross." The Princeton Recollector. August 1981.

"Matthews Construction Demanded Best Workmanship." The Princeton Recollector. Autumn, 1978.

"The Princeton Herald's Poll Revealed Strong Approval of the Square." The Princeton Recollector. Autumn 1978.

"Princeton History Set Stone on Stone by Fiabane." The Princeton Recollector. September 1979.

"Troopers Still At Lindbergh's: Three Have 'Kept House' In Nearby Place Since Night of the Kidnapping." Unidentified Newspaper. September 22, [1933].

Berg, A . Scott. Lindbergh: A Biography. GP Putnam's Sons, NY. 1998.

Cafaro, Jeanette. E-mail correspondence with author. January 24, 2008.

Lindbergh, Anne Morrow. Hour of Gold, Hour of Lead: The Diaries of Anne Morrow Lindbergh 1929 – 1932. Harcourt Brace Jovanovich, NY. 1973.

Highfields: Albert Elias RGC. Amwell Heritage Society, Ringoes, NJ. C. 1994.

Springer, Irene. Interview with author. January 2001.

Lindbergh, Anne Morrow. "Locked Rooms and Open Doors." Harcourt Brace Jovanovich, NY. 1974.

Lindbergh, Anne Morrow. "The Flower and the Nettle." Harcourt Brace Jovanovich, NY. 1976.

Lindbergh, Anne Morrow. "War Within and Without." Harcourt Brace Jovanovich, NY. 1980.

Woolfolk, Ann. Interview with William Fiabane. Princeton Historical Society, 1982.

9. Al Reich

"Al Reich Cleared of Faking In a Bout." New York Times. February 3, 1915.

"Al Reich Victor in Three Rounds." New York Times. December17, 1915.

"Boxing Fans Hoot Tame Bout at Rink." New York Times. October 15, 1915

"Cyclists In Good Shape." New York Times. November 23, 1914.

Cyber Boxing Zone. www.cyberboxingzone.com/boxing/reich-a.htm

Cyber Boxing Zone. www.cyberboxingzone.com/boxing/w-hope.htm

Reich, Al. Testimony. State of New Jersey vs. Bruno Richard Hauptmann Trial Transcripts. 1935.

Reich, Alfred J. Obituary. Unknown Newspaper. July 24, 1963.

Reich, Alfred J. Statement. May 13, 1932.

Walsh, Harry. May 18th 1932 Conference.

10. Betty Gow

Bornmann, Louis J. and Frank Carr. Report. New Jersey State Police. "Information on Betty Gow." R718. June 15, 1932.

Cullen, Thomas F. "Betty Gow and Sailor Friend Cleared in Lindy Kidnap Quiz." Unknown Newspaper. December 15, 1933.

Gow, Betty. Birth Certificate. February 12, 1904.

Gow, Betty. Death Certificate. July 16, 1996.

Gow, Betty. Statement. March 3, 1932 (first).

Gow, Betty. Statement. March 3, 1932 (second).

Gow, Betty. Statement. March 10, 1932.

Gow, Betty. Statement. March 12, 1932.

Gow, Betty. Statement. May 13, 1932.

Gow, Betty. Certificate of Admission of Alien. New York. March 10, 1932.

Innes, Robert. Report. "Betty Gow." City of Glasgow Police. November 5, 1934.

Mac? [illegible], Adam. Letter. City of Glasgow Police.

Taylor, Isabella Anderson [Gow]. Death Certificate. March 6, 1969.

11. Olly & Elsie Whateley

"Lindbergh Visits Butler, Seriously Ill at Princeton After Operation." Unknown Newspaper. March 22, 1933.

Bornmann, Louis J. Report. R112. re: Interviewing Ambrose Titus and Wife. March 12, 1932.

Conklin, William S. Memorandum to Governor Harold G. Hoffman. Re: Inquiring into the reported death of Phoebe Elsie Whateley. December 2, 1937.

Jempson, F. J. Correspondence. Birmingham City Police to Metropolitan Police (New Scotland Yard). March 5, 1932.

Whateley, Elsie Marie. Statement. March 10, 1932.

Whateley, Elsie Marie. Testimony. State of New Jersey vs. Bruno Richard Hauptmann Trial Transcripts. 1935.

Whateley, Olly. Death Certificate. May 23, 1933.

Whateley, Olly. Obituary. Unknown Newspaper. May 24, 1933.

Whateley, Olly. Statement. March 3, 1932.

12. Septimus Banks

Adriatic, RMS. Manifest. 10 September 1922. http://www. ellisisland. org/

Banks, Rose. Death Certificate. November 21, 1929. Department of Health of the City of New York, Bureau of Records

Banks, Septimus S. Social Security Account Application. U. S. Social Security Administration, April 27, 1939.

Banks, Septimus S. Social Security Death Master File. RootsWeb. com, Inc. http://ssdi. genealogy. rootsweb. com/

Delerium Tremens. EMedicine from WebbMD. http://www. emedicine. com/EMERG/topic123. htm

Hertog, Susan. Anne Morrow Lindbergh: Her Life. Doubleday, New York: 1999.

Lusitania, RMS. Manifest. 18 September 1914. http://www. ellisisland. org/

Milton, Joyce. Loss of Eden: A Biography of Charles and Anne Morrow Lindbergh. HarperCollins, New York: 1993.

Seykora, J. E. Report. US Department of Justice. 5/10/34. New Jersey State Police Lindbergh Files. Files, F-447.

Seykora, J. E. Report. US Department of Justice. 5/18/34. New Jersey State Police Lindbergh Files, F-447.

Sisk, T. H. Summary Report. US Department of Justice. 1 February 1934.

13. Colonel Henry Breckinridge

"Asked Wilson's Support; Would Not Accept Federalized Militia in Lieu of Continental Army." New York Times. February 11, 1916

"Breckinridge Asks Better Defenses." New York Times. June 1, 1915.

"Breckinridge Fighting Him: Votes for New York Man May Be Labeled as Anti-Roosevelt." Charleston Daily Mail. April 21, 1936.

"Breckinridge, Hall, Piti and Nunes Lead Foilsmen in Title Tourney Bouts; Breckinridge May Be Olympic Fencer." New York Times. April 28, 1920.

"Breckinridge Out To Fight New Deal." New York Times. September 3, 1934

"Divorces Henry Breckinridge." New York Times. March 28, 1947.

"Col. Breckinridge Will Lead U. S. Fencers Into Action Against British Team Here." New York Times. March 4, 1926.

"Fencing in Washington: Six Women Members of Reorganized Club Give Exhibition." New York Times. January 25, 1914.

"Get $415,000 Gold to London Refugees: Removed in Kegs from Tennessee and Rushed in Bullion Car to Needy Americans." New York Times. August 18, 1914.

"Henry Breckinridge Seeks Reno Divorce." New York Times. February 18, 1947.

"Name Breckinridge as Fencing Captain." New York Times. January 30, 1928.

"Shot Kills Daughter of Col. Breckinridge; Girl, 17, Discharges Own Rifle by Accident." New York Times. July 21, 1934.

"US Secretary of War Resigns." This Day In History. February 10, 1916. http://www.history.com/this-day-in-history.do?id=212&tion=tdihArticleCategory

"Washington Team Wins Epee Title: Captures National Championship in Dueling Sword Contest at Fencers' Club." New York Times. April 21, 1921.

Berg, A. Scott. "Lindbergh." G. P. Putnam's Sons, NY. 1998.

Breckinridge, Aida. Obituary. New York Times. May 29, 1962.

Breckinridge Family History. http://www. breckinridge.com/breckbio. htm

Breckinridge, Henry. Obituary. New York Times. May 3, 1960.

Breckinridge, Henry. Obituary. http://www. historicpatterson.org/Exhibits/ExhMiscellaneous.php

Database of Olympics. http://www.databaseofolympics.com/players/playerpage.htm?id=BRECKHEN01

Hess, Stephen. "America's Political Dynasties." Transaction Publishers, 1997

Lindbergh, Anne Morrow. "Hour of Gold, Hour of Lead." Harcourt Brace Jovanovich, NY. 1973.

Lindbergh, Anne Morrow. "The Flower and the Nettle." Harcourt Brace Jovanovich, NY. 1976.

Lindbergh, Anne Morrow. "War Within and Without." Harcourt Brace Jovanovich, NY. 1980.

Milton, Joyce. "Loss of Eden." Harper Collins, NY. 1993.

Mosley, Leonard. "Lindbergh: A Biography." Dover Publications Re-Issue Edition. March 2000.

Our Campaigns http://www.ourcampaigns.com/CandidateDetail.html?CandidateID=18814

Parmalee, T. A. "A Biography of President Woodrow Wilson." http://ball.tcnj. edu/pols370/wilson. htm

Ruiz, Vicki L. and Virginia Sánchez Korrol. "Latinas in the United States: A Historical Encyclopedia." Indiana University Press, 2006.

Schwarzkopf, H. Norman. Memo for File. March 22, 1932. HGH Box 26 "Eberhard."

Tinling, Marion. "Women Remembered: A Guide to Landmarks of Women's History in the United States." Greenwood Press, 1986.

US Fencing Hall Of Fame. http://fencingonfairfield. com/halloffame/index. php?option-com_content&task=view&id=29&Itemid=28.

Women in Transportation: Changing America's History. US Department of Transportation Federal Highway Administration. March 1998. http:// www. fhwa. dot. gov/ohim/wmntrans2. pdf

14. The Norfolk Triumvirate of Intermediaries

"Careers of Negotiators: Curtis, Peacock and Burrage Have Led Active Lives." New York Times. March 30, 1932.

"Colonel Lindbergh's Testimony Under Cross-Examination at the Hoax Trial." New York Times. June 29, 1932.

"Flies to Lindbergh to Report Contact with Kidnappers." New York Times. March 29, 1932.

"Lindbergh Hoax Figure Asks Rights of Pardon. New York Times. September 1,1937.

"Named to British Church." New York Times. January 19, 1936.

Annas, Teresa. "Meet the Architect Behind Norfolk Church Addition Controversy." The Virginian-Pilot. September 25, 2006. http:// hamptonroads. com/node/159011

Burrage, Admiral Guy. Obituary. New York Times. June 18, 1954.

Curtis, John Hughes. Statement. May 14, 1932.

Curtis, John Hughes. Report of Questioning. May 17, 1932

Fisher, C. Lloyd. The Case New Jersey Would Like To Forget. "Part One: A Southern Gentleman and an Enigma Named Sam." Liberty. August 1, 1936.

Fisher, C. Lloyd. The Case New Jersey Would Like To Forget. "Part Two: The Gang Tells Its Story." Liberty. August 8, 1936.

Fisher, C. Lloyd. The Case New Jersey Would Like To Forget. "Part Seven: Conclusion." Liberty. September 12, 1936.

Historic Congressional Cemetery. "Navy Yard Tour – 12th Stop." http://www. congressionalcemetery. org/Education/Tours/NavyYard/NavyTour_12th. html

Richard, G. L. "List of Flights made By Myself with J. H. Curtis and Dean H. Dobson-Peacock." US Naval Air Station, Norfolk, Virginia. May 19, 1932.

Whiting, K. Captain. "Flights Made By Captain Whiting and Party…In Connection with the Yacht Marcon.." US Naval Air Station, Norfolk, Virginia. [1932].

15. H. Norman Schwarzkopf

"Soldier, Policeman, Statesman." Triangle. January/February 1959. Vol 2 No 1. Page 1.

Boehm, Sid. "Faith to Lindy Sealed My Lips – Schwarzkopf." New York Evening Journal. February 16, 1935.

Coakley, Leo J. "Jersey Troopers: A Fifty Year History of the New Jersey State Police." Rutgers University Press, New Brunswick, NJ. 1971.

Falzini, Mark. "Mission to Iran." Archival Ramblings. April 2007. http:// njspmuseum.blogspot. com/2007/03/mission-to-iran_120. html

Falzini, Mark. "The State Police in 1932." Archival Ramblings. December 2007. http://njspmuseum.blogspot.com/2007/12/state-police-in-1932. html

New Jersey State Police. Biographical Sketch. Teletype. [November 1958].

Schwarzkopf, H. Norman. Obituary. New York Times. November 28, 1958.

16. Hugo Stockburger

Stockburger, Hugo. Interview with author. January 21, 2005.

Stockburger, Hugo. Scrapbook. New Jersey State Police Museum.

17. The State Police Investigators

Lewis Bornmann

Bergner, G. W. Letter. May 29, 1931.

Bornmann, Lewis J. Application for enlistment. 1926.

Bornmann, Lewis J. Letter (requesting reduction in rank). [no date]

Bornmann, Lewis J. Letter. July 31, 1951.

Bornmann, Lewis J. Personnel Information Card

Bornmann, Lewis J. Personnel Information Sheet, October 10, 1946; February 2, 1951.

Bornmann, Lewis J. Request for permission to marry. August 10, 1930.

Bornmann, Lewis J. Request for Transfer, January 6, 1931

Memorandum 133, September 28, 1937.

Personnel Order 165, August 29, 1952

Schwarzkopf, H. Norman. Letter. June 5, 1931.

Special Order 48, December 1, 1928

Special Order 71, April 5, 1928

Special Order 311, May 1, 1930

Special Order 160, June 1, 1931

Special Order 70, December 14, 1931

Special Order 125, June 27, 1932

Special Order 125, July 1, 1932

Special Order 453, June 6, 1936

Special Order 146, November 19, 1941

Special Order 146, December 1, 1941

Special Order 221, May 27, 1942

Special Order 221, June 1, 1942

Special Order 1, July 1, 1947

Special Order 104, October 30, 1947

Special Order 104, December 1, 1947

Special Order 39, February 28, 1951

John Wallace

"Simeon Stylites." Bergen Evening Record. June 1930.

"State Policeman Hackensack Chief." Jersey Journal. November 18, 1929.

"To Name New Chief." Bergen Evening Record. July 3, 1930.

Kelly, David B. Letter. October 21, 1971.

Personnel Order 25, January 31, 1949

Personnel Order 92, July 1, 1949

Special Order 124, April 20, 1925

Special Order 35, October 20, 1926

Special Order 56, February 25, 1927

Special Order 86, March 3, 1927

Special Order 18, August 23, 1927

Special Order 37, March 3, 1927

Special Order 48, December 31, 1927

Special Order 48, January 1, 1928

Special Order 69, April 4, 1928

Special Order 70, April 5, 1928

Special Order 205, November 29, 1929

Special Order 332, June 19, 1930

Special Order 332, July 1, 1930

Special Order 125, June 27, 1932

Special Order 125, July 1, 1932

Special Order 460, July 16, 1932

Special Order 369, May 5, 1934

Special Order 296, July 26, 1934

Special Order 309, September 5, 1934

Special Order 454, June 6, 1936

Special Order 460, July 1, 1936

Special Order 426, April 16, 1945

Special Order 75, January 29, 1949

Wallace, John. Application for enlistment. 1924.

Wallace, John. Change of marital status. March 21, 1942.

Wallace, John. Letter. January 18, 1964.

Wallace, John. Letter. April 17, 1967.

Wallace, John. Personnel Information Card, 1951.

Wallace, John. Request for leave of absence. July 10, 1936.

Wallace, John. Request to marry. June 11, 1926.

Wallace, John. Request to marry. July 27, 1934.

Wallace, John. Request to marry. July 11, 1942.

Wallace, John. Resignation. July 16, 1926.

Wallace, John. Social Security Death Index. http://ssdi. genealogy. rootsweb. com/

Wallace, John. Summary of career. August 29, 1952.

Joseph Wolf

Dunn, Arthur C. Letter of Commendation. July 3, 1935.

Dunn, Daniel. Letter of Recommendation. December 30, 1949.

Dunn, Daniel. Subject/To Letter. October 28, 1941.

Elmendorf, C. H. Special Report of Investigation. March 3, 1928.

Patterson, Claude. Special Report of Investigation. March 1, 1928.

Personnel Order 17, January 25, 1949

Personnel Order 92, July 1, 1949

Personnel Order 93, July 1, 1949

Personnel Order 146, October 1, 1953

Personnel Order 37, March 31, 1955

Personnel Order 89, July 7, 1955

Personnel Order 8, January 30, 1956

Special Order 88, March 5, 1931

Special Order 103, March 30, 1931

Special Order 125, June 27, 1932

Special Order 337, June 11, 1935

Special Order 412, September 7, 1935

Special Order 146, November 19, 1941

Wolf, Joseph. Application for enlistment. 1928.

Wolf, Joseph. Personnel Information Card.

Wolf, Joseph. Personnel Information Sheet, July 17, 1956.

Wolf, Joseph. Social Security Death Index. http://ssdi. genealogy. rootsweb. com/

Wolf, Joseph. Subject/To Letter. May 23, 1953.

William Horn

Fisher, Jim. "The Lindbergh Case." Rutgers University Press, New Brunswick. 1987.

Horn, William. Application for enlistment. 1927.

Horn, William. Discharge Papers [State Police]. March 15, 1929

Horn, William. Fingerprint Card.

Horn, William. Personnel Information Card.

Horn, William. Personnel Information Sheet, October 28, 1946.

Horn, William. Request for reinstatement. December 27, 1929.

Horn, William. Resignation. August 31, 1929.

Horn, William. Social Security Death Index. http://ssdi. genealogy. rootsweb. com/

Personnel Order 1, July 1, 1947

Personnel Order 154, October 5, 1949

Renkine, H. T. Special Investigation Report. March 6, 1927.

Special Order 71, April 5, 1928

Special Order 34, October 1, 1928

Special Order 288, April 1, 1930

Special Order 27, September 1, 1931

Special Order 453, June 6, 1936

Special Order 161, January 19, 1942

Special Order 409, September 5, 1935

Special Order 161, January 19, 1942.

Andrew Zapolsky

Brettell, Richard. Letter. October 26, 1936.

Carter, William. Subject/To Letter. July 7, 1930.

Fox, Daniel. Letter. September 1, 1935.

Mathel, W. H. Letter. March 13, 1935.

Tupper, F. H. Letter. July 9, 1935.

Personnel Order 1, July 1, 1947

Personnel Order 33, February 19, 1951

Personnel Order 22, March 4, 1952

Personnel Order 48, April 1, 1952

Personnel Order 148, August 6, 1952

Snook, Russell. Letter. October 29, 1952

Special Order 42, November 26, 1927

Special Order 87, March 15, 1929.

Special Order 84, February 2, 1931

Special Order 85, February 27, 1931

Special Order 152, May 26, 1931

Special Order 155, May 26, 1931

Zapolsky, Andrew. Application for enlistment. August 15, 1927.

Zapolsky, Andrew. Application for retirement. January 9, 1953.

Zapolsky, Andrew. Certificate As To Service and Final Salary. January 9, 1953.

Zapolsky, Andrew. Personnel Card. [1946]

Zapolsky, Andrew. Personnel Information Sheet. January 31, 1951.

Zapolsky, Andrew. Request for Disability Pension. July 15, 1952.

Zapolsky, Andrew. Subject/To Letter. July 1952.

Zapolsky, Andrew. Subject/To Letter. October 8, 1952.

Zapolsky, Andrew. Subject/To Letter. June 5, 1956.

Arthur T. Keaten

"Schwarzkopf Men Shifted in New Jersey." New York Times. July 16,1936.

Carter, William. Memo. September 24, 1925.

Carter, William. Subject/To Letter. August 7, 1925.

Keaten, Arthur T. Application for enlistment. . October 1, 1922.

Keaten, Arthur T. Application for Retirement. March 28, 1956.

Keaten, Arthur T. Birth Certificate.

Keaten, Arthur T. Personnel Card.

Keaten, Arthur T. Personnel Sheet. November 6, 1954.

Keaten, Arthur T. Request to marry. September 27, 1927.

Keaten, Arthur T. Request for Transfer. July 4, 1925.

Keaten, Arthur T. Social Security Death Index. http://ssdi. genealogy. rootsweb. com/

Keaten, Arthur T. Jr and Lydia [Jr]. Thank You Card. [December 1992]

New Jersey State Police. Triangle. [1991]

Personnel Order 40, May 16, 1956

Personnel Order 22, March 4, 1952

Personnel Order 46, April 1, 1952

Schwarzkopf, H. Norman. Letter. January 23, 1930

Special Order 171, August 7, 1925

Special Order 87, March 3, 1927

Special Order 44, November 30, 1927

Special Order 69, April 4, 1928

Special Order 71, April 5, 1928

Special Order 70, May 5, 1928

Special Order 128, May 20, 1928

Special Order 241, January 21, 1930

Special Order 4, July 1, 1930

Special Order 252, March 7, 1934

Special Order 450, July 16, 1936

Special Order 99, August 30, 1941

Special Order 112, October 1, 1941

Special Order 255, February 23, 1944

Special Order 426, April 16, 1945

Special Order 182, April 29, 1947

Eugene Haussling

"Drops Name Germania: Fire Insurance Company Is Now the National Liberty." New York Times. March 1, 1918.

Haussling, Eugene. Personnel Card.

Haussling, Eugene. Application for enlistment. 1923.

Haussling, Eugene. Enlistment Papers. April 1, 1923.

Haussling, Eugene. "Famed State Police Detective Retires Today. Trenton Sunday Times. February 25, 1951.

Personnel Order 52, March 29, 1951

Special Order 83, July 27, 1923

Special Order 256, May 1, 1926

Special Order 76, March 1, 1927

Special Order 101, April 1, 1927

Special Order 9, August 15, 1927

Special Order 175, October 1, 1929

Special Order 288, April 1, 1930

Special Order 10, July 10, 1930.

Special Order 453, June 6, 1936.

Special Order 136, February 15, 1943

Teletype 241 File 3 SP Colts Neck re: Natural Death Retired Member New Jersey State Police." March 21, 1970

Teletype 976 File 14 SP Princeton re: 241 File 3 SP Colts Neck Death of Retired Member E. Haussling. March 22, 1970.

Samuel J. Leon

Dies, Martin Jr. Biographical Guide to the US Congress.

http://bioguide. congress. gov/scripts/biodisplay. pl?index=D000338

Kladko, Brian. "Sam Leon, Lindbergh Prober, Dies at 81." Courier-News. June 10, 1985.

Leon, Samuel J. Personnel Card.

Leon, Samuel J. Application for enlistment. 1926.

Leon, Samuel J. Personnel Information Sheet. January 3, 1958.

Personnel Order 25, March 5, 1958

John J. Lamb

Hogan, Timothy. Obituary. New York Times. August 26, 1899.

Lamb, John J. Personnel Card.

Lamb, John J. Application for enlistment. 1921.

Lamb, John J. Obituary. New York Times. June 8, 1940.

New Jersey State Police. Funeral Teletype. . June 1940.

Special Order 18. March 26, 1924.

Special Order 118, June 3, 1932.

Special Order 396, August 1, 1935.

Special Order 821, June 7, 1940.

Nuncio DeGaetano

Bruno, Anthony. "All About Frank Sinatra and the Mob." Crime Library. http://www. crimelibrary. com/gangsters_outlaws/cops_others/frank_sinatra/2. html

Coakley, Leo. "Jersey Troopers: A Fifty Year History of the New Jersey State Police." Rutgers University Press, New Brunswick. 1971.

DeGaetano, Nuncio. Application for Enlistment. 1929.

DeGaetano, Nuncio. Personnel Card.

DeGaetano, Nuncio. Report re: Anticipating Complaint from Warden McCrea of the Hunterdon County Jail. January 25, 1935.

DeGaetano, Nuncio. Personnel Information Sheet. October 4, 1954.

Gardner, Lloyd C. "The Case That Never Dies: The Lindbergh Kidnapping." Rutgers University Press, New Brunswick. 2004.

Leon, Samuel J. Special Report. February 25, 1929.

Personnel Inter-Office Communication. July 21, 1955.

Personnel Order 125, June 27, 1932.

Personnel Order 1, July 1, 1947.

Personnel Order 31, March 17, 1952.

Personnel Order 139, July 8, 1953.

Personnel Order 88, July 5, 1955.

Special Order 113, April 1, 1931.

Special Order 53, November 2, 1931.

18. William Allen

"Allen Back At Work: Negro Who Found Baby's Body Embarrassed by Cameras." New York Times. May 14, 1932.

"Negro Tells How He Found Body in Woods; 'Nothing Too Bad for the Man That Did It.'" New York Times. May 13, 1932.

"William Allen. Lindberg Baby Finder?" From the collection of the Allen Family. Author and date unknown.

Allen, William. Obituary. New York Times. December 22, 1965.

Allen, William. Social Security Death Database. http://ssdi.genealogy. rootsweb. com/

Allen, William. Statement. May 12, 1932.

Allen, William Jr. Interview with author. 2006.

Buckingham County, Virginia. "A History of Buckingham County." http:// www. buckinghamcountyva. org/history/historyofbuckingham. html

Ganie, Elinor. Biographical Essay About William Allen. [date unknown].

Ganie, Elinor. Telephone interview. March 4, 2008.

Miller, Rich. "Bad News Prevails in 1930." New York Times. c. 1999

Pulaski Skyway. http://www. nycroads. com/crossings/pulaski/

Titus, Livingston. Statement. May 12, 1932.

Wilson, Orville. Statement. May 12, 1932.

19. Violet Sharp

"A Church Near You – Beenham: St. Mary, Berkshire." http://www. acny. org. uk/venue. php?V-518

Chetwode, Lady Hester. Letter of Recommendation. August 1, 1929.

Cornels, Katherine. Interview. June 12, 1933.

Garnsey, Mary Sharp. Marriage Certificate.

Payne, George. Death Certificate.

Payne, George. Statement. June 17, 1932.

Payne, George. Will. June 15, 1942.

Randall, Leslie. Telegram. June 11, 1932.

Sharp, Emily/Edna. Statement. January 26, 1933.

Sharp, George. Marriage Certificate.

Sharp, James. Birth Certificate.

Sharp, James. Letter. September 10, 1931.

Sharp, Lucy. Death Certificate.

Sharp, Lucy. Letter. [undated]

Sharp, Lucy. Letter [undated]

Sharp, Violet. Certificate of Registry of Birth. July 25, 1904.

Sharp, Violet. Entry of Birth (certified copy). July 25, 1904.

Shephard, G. Acting British Consul General. Letter. June 17, 1932

Simmons, Fan. Letter. 1932.

Telegram. Unsigned and no date. "Governor Moore Announced This Afternoon…"

Waller, Ian H. Violet Sharp Report. February 2008.

Webb, Nellie L. Letter of Recommendation. August 7, 1929

20. Associate Justice Thomas W. Trenchard

"Burglars Rob Justice Trenchard." New York Times. April 3, 1916

"Court of Oyer and Terminer." http://www. nj. gov/state/darm/links/webcat/queries/sjoyer. htm

"Hauptmann Panel to be Picked Today." New York Times. November 27, 1934

"Hauptmann Trial to be Hard Fought." New York Times. December 30, 1934.

"Mrs. T. W. Trenchard; Wife of Supreme Court Justice of New Jersey Dies in Trenton." New York Times. February 10, 1938.

"Noted Justice Presided at Trial of Bruno Hauptmann." Unidentified Newspaper.

Trenchard Collection, New Jersey State Police Museum.

"Rites for Ex-Judge Trenchard." New York Times. July 28, 1942.

"T. W. Trenchard, Hauptmann Judge…Dies at Home in Trenton." New York Times. July 24, 1942.

"Trenchard, 77, Ends Service on Jersey Bench." Unidentified Newspaper. Trenchard Collection, New Jersey State Police Museum.

Classic Encyclopedia. New Jersey – Administration – Judicial System. http://www1911encylopedia. org/New_Jersey

Fisher, Jim. "The Lindbergh Case." Rutgers University Press. 1987.

Hallam, Oscar. "Report of Special Committee on Publicity in Criminal Trials." American Bar Association. April 9,1936.

Hallam, Oscar. "Some Object Lessons on Publicity in Criminal Trials." Minnesota Law Review. Journal of the State Bar Association. Vol. 24 No. 4. March 1940.

Hann, Elmer Ellsworth. Obituary. Unidentified Newspaper. February 25, 1937.

Hardyman, James. Letter to Thomas Trenchard. January 15, 1935.

Kennedy, Ludovic. "The Airman and the Carpenter." Viking Press, 1985.

Kilgallen, James L. "Two Distinguished Justices…" International News Service. December 11, 1934.

Mitchell, Joseph M. "Crier Calls Terminer 'Terminal' And Justice Gets His Daily Laugh." World-Telegram. January 30, 1935. Sackett, William E. "Modern Battles of Trenton." Volume II. The Neale Publishing Company, NY. 1914.

Scannell, John James. "Scannell's New Jersey's First Citizens and State Guide." Paterson, NJ. 1919.

Trenchard, Thomas Whitaker. Find A Grave Memorial. http://wwwfindagrave. com/cgi-bin/fg. cgi?page-gr&Grid=6391566

21. The Talesmen of Flemington

"44 ½ Average Age of Hauptmann Jury." World-Telegram. January 4, 1935.

"Birthday Cake Adds to Menu of Bruno Jury." New York American. January 19, 1935.

"Bruno's Jurors Met Again and None Is Guilty of Humor." Evening Journal. Date unknown.

"CCC Juryman Last to Vote For Death." Newspaper unknown. February 14, 1935.

"Foreman of Jury 25 Years in Same Job; Nine of the First Ten Chosen Have Families." New York Times. January 2, 1935.

"Hauptmann Juror Dies." New York Times. December 30, 1935.

"Hauptmann Juror Killed." New York Times. May 9, 1935.

"Hauptmann Juror Recalls 'Pact'." March 7, 1985. Miller Scrapbook #9.

"Hauptmann Jurors Expect $129 But Hope For $258." Newark News. Date unknown.

"Hauptmann Jurors Plan Annual Fete: Will Discuss Permanent Organization When Trial Ends, Says Constable." Associated Press. February 13, 1935.

"Hauptmann Jurors Take a Constitutional." Evening Journal. Date unknown.

"Hauptmann Jury." Associated Press. January 3, 1935.

"The Historical Marker Database." Taylor Wharton Iron and Steel Company Marker. http://www. hmdb. org/Marker. asp?Marker=5041

"Juror Tells of Deliberations." New York Sun. February 15, 1935.

"Jurors Live in Seclusion." Newark Star Eagle. January 31, 1935.

"Jurors Play Cards In Leisure Time." Associated Press. January 3, 1935.

"Jurors Show Mixed Feelings Listening to Mrs. Hauptmann." New York Evening Sun. January 31, 1935.

"Jury Heavyweights Gain Poundage." Newark Star Eagle. January 14, 1935.

"Mince Pie Upsets Juror: Mrs. Snyder Falls From Bed." Brooklyn Daily Eagle. January 31, 1935.

"Sidelights on the Big Trial…" Newspaper unknown. January 30, 1935.

"There Are The Jurors Who Hold Bruno Hauptmann's Fate In Their Hands." New York American. February 14, 1935.

"Third Hauptmann Juror Dies." New York Times. January 22, 1941.

"Three Women Jurors Remove Hats; Fourth Sits Bundled in Coat." Newspaper unknown. January 5, 1935.

"Treat Bruno Juror For Heart Attack." Associated Press. January 26, 1935.

"Two Jurors Are Ill: 261-lb Woman Ate Too Much." Newspaper unknown. January 26, 1935.

"Valley People's Names Drawn For Hauptmann Jury." Delaware Valley News. November 30, 1934.

"What a Juror Does on a Day Off." New York American. 1935.

"'Why We Convicted Hauptmann': Jurors For First Time Give Reasons For Their Verdict of Guilty." New York Journal. June 24, 1935.

1930 Census. Califon Borough, Hunterdon County, New Jersey.

Bar Association of Nassau County. Invitation. February 25, 1937.

Carroll, George. "Woman Juror Aided Former Prosecutor." New York Evening Journal. February 11, 1935.

Conway, Robert. "Woman Juror Cheers Bruno With a Smile." The News. January 29, 1935.

DeWolf, Rose. "Lindbergh Kidnapping: The Case They Never Forgot: Central Figures Recall it With Lingering Grief." Newspaper unknown. January 2, 1965.

Donoghue, William J. "Jury Gets Offer to Stage Bruno Vote in Theatres." [New York Evening Journal]. February 15, 1935.

Donoghue, William. "Offer for 12 to Appear on Stage Tour Confirmed by Foreman." New York Evening Journal. February 16, 1935.

Donoghue, William J. "Wife of Jury Foreman Thinks Bruno Guilty." New York Evening Journal. February 11, 1935

Fuerst, Liz. "Jury Foreman Discusses Hauptmann Trial: Walton Recalls 46 Days Spent In Court, Hotel." Newspaper unknown. March 4, 1976.

Ghent, Ray. "Reaction of Jury Is Trial Mystery." Newark Star Eagle. January 14, 1935.

Haslett, J. W. "Each Juror a Specialist to Weigh Bits of Evidence." World-Telegram. February 13, 1935.

Killgallen, Dorothy. "Hauptmann Jurors Represent Cross-Section of Country Life." [New York Journal-American?] January 9, 1935.

Levitt, Robert D. "Goose Hangs High as Bruno's Jury Holds Flemington Reunion." Date and newspaper unknown.

Mack, Ed. "Hauptmann Juror Curious About Evidence." Newspaper unknown. January 31, 1935.

Mitchell, Joseph M. "Crier Calls Terminer 'Terminal' And Justice Gets His Daily Laugh." World-Telegram. January 30, 1935.

Neliz, Cirilo. Correspondence to Miss. Ethel Stockton. February 13, 1935.

New Jersey State Police Report. R1600. Selection of 48 persons for Pettit Jury service on trial of State of New Jersey vs Bruno Richard Hauptmann. R1600. December 26, 1934.

Osterout, Howard. Correspondence to Mrs. Elmer [Ethel] Stockton. February 16, 1937.

Snyder, Mrs. F. P. Obituary. December 31, 1974. Miller Scrapbook #11.

St. Johns, Adela Rogers. "Experts' Battle Puts Jury In Spotlight." International News Service. February 1, 1935.

Walton, Charles. Obituary. September 24, 1981. Miller Scrapbook #8.

Winchell, Walter. "Smasho! Flash! Crash!!!" New York Daily Mirror. January 30, 1935.

22. The Experts

"The History of Fingerprints." http://onin. com/fp/fphistory. html.

Hudson, Erastus Mead. Obituary. New York Times. September 17, 1943.

Koehler, Arthur. Obituary. United States Forest Products Laboratory. July 17, 1967.

Osborn, Albert D. Obituary. New York Times. October 29, 1972.

Osborn, Albert S. Obituary. New York Times. December 16, 1946.

Schoenfeld, Dudley. Obituary. New York Times. September 28, 1971.

23. C. Lloyd Fisher

"Camp Foran-Fisher." http://www.cnjc-sa.org/council/history/ooc/campforan/index. htm.

"C. Lloyd Fisher is Cleared." New York Times. July 30, 1937.

"Fastest Talker is Lloyd Fisher." Unidentified Newspaper. 1935.

"Fisher Belittles Prosecutor Bid." Sunday Times. February 14, 1937.

"Hauptmann Lawyer Named Prosecutor." New York Times. May 25, 1937.

"Jersey Faces Rise in Milk & Cream." New York Times. November 29, 1942.

"Large Attendance At Funeral Service For Lloyd Fisher." Unidentified Newspaper. July 1960.

"Lloyd Fisher Town Hero." Unidentified Newspaper. 1935.

Berg, A. Scott. "Lindbergh." G. P. Putnam's Sons, NY. 1998.

Blackman, Samuel G. "Jersey's Famous Case Haunting." Sunday Times Advertiser. February 27, 1972.

Fisher, C. Lloyd. Obituary. New York Times. July 1, 1960.

Fisher, Jim. "The Lindbergh Case." Rutgers University Press. 1987.

Kennedy, Ludovic. "The Airman and the Carpenter." Viking Press, 1985.

Mitchell, Joseph M. "Crier Calls Terminer 'Terminal' And Justice Gets His Daily Laugh." World-Telegram. January 30, 1935.

24. Frederick Pope

"Confesses He Shot Ellis For a Woman." New York Times. January 17, 1914.

"Detained Carl's Aunt." New York Times. January 19, 1914.

"Frederick A. Pope Retained to Assist Hauptmann Defense." Unknown Newspaper December 6, 1934.

"F. A. Pope Sworn as Judge." New York Times. March 14, 1935.

Pope, Frederick Allen. Obituary. New York Times. June 23, 1952.

25. Egbert Rosecrans

"City Counsel Arrested." New York Times. November 1, 1923.

Rosecrans, Egbert. Obituary. New York Times.

January 21, 1948.

26. Anthony M. Hauck, Jr.

"Anthony Hauck Dies, Noted County Lawyer." [Hunterdon County Democrat?]. September 1972.

"Geologist Is Accused: Held in Moral Offense Against Girl Who Shot Him." New York Times, May 10, 1957.

"Girl Ruled Delinquent: Sandra Hauck Faces Further Inquiry in Jersey Shooting." New York Times, May 25, 1957.

"Shooting By Girl, 15, Called No Accident." New York Times, April 5, 1957.

Burke, Hollis. "Death Revives Trial Memories." Unknown Newspaper. September 1972.

Stoelting v. Hauck, 32 N. J. 87, 159 A. 2d 385 (N. J., 1960).